Musicmakers
of
West Africa

John Collins

Musicmakers
of
West Africa

John Collins

3CP

An Original by Three Continents

©John Collins 1985

First Edition

Three Continents Press
1346 Connecticut Avenue NW
Washington, DC 20036

ISBN: 0-89410-075-0
ISBN: 0-89410-076-9 (pbk)
LC No: 81-51651

Cover design by Norman Ware
Cover drawing, "Right On, Brother," ©Obiora Udechukwu

Contents

Photographs

All photos courtesy of the author, except those of Haruna Ishola and *The Funkees,* courtesy of *Music Express,* Lagos; and that of Bunny Mack, courtesy of Afrodisc, Ltd., London.

Introduction

This book is a collection of essays and interviews I have written on the West African music scene over a period of years. I have placed them in rough chronological order from the early dance band and guitar band period through Pop music and the situation today. To help the reader who is unfamiliar with this subject, the following introduction will act as a framework for the various chapters and give continuity to them.

The Beginnings of Highlife

Highlife grew out of the music styles present in the coastal towns of West Africa during the last century, which led to a fusion of indigenous dance rhythms and melodies with influences from the West. One source of this outside influence was from the regimental bands associated with the forts and composed of European-trained African musicians; these played military marches, Polkas and popular ballads of the time. Another source was the sea shanties and folksongs introduced by sailors of every nationality, including black seamen from the West Indies and Americas. In fact some of the earliest Highlife was played on a combination of African percussion instruments and sailors' instruments like the guitar, concertina and harmonica. Finally, there was the effect of the piano music and church hymns of the educated elite.

By the beginning of the century, these foreign influences at work in the local music scene led to a number of "proto-Highlife" styles such as the Osibisaba of the Fantis of southwestern Ghana, the Ashiko and Gome (Gombe) music of the Accra people, the "Dagomba" guitar

1

songs of Liberian sailors, and Creole melodies from Sierra Leone. By the First World War period these became known collectively as Highlife, and all contained two basic rhythms. Most were in duple or four-four time and the others, referred to as "Blues," were in six-eight time.

The Inter-War Period

By the 1920s, Highlife had become firmly established, especially in Ghana where it was played by three distinct types of bands. One was the brass and fife band. Any town of note in southern Ghana would only be satisfied if they had such a band to play regimental marches and Highlifes at Empire Day parades, picnics and other town functions. The large towns like Accra, Cape Coast and Kumasi also had prestigious ballroom orchestras which played Waltzes, Foxtrots, Quicksteps, Ragtimes, Rumbas, and Highlifes to a black elite audience in top hats and evening dress. The earliest of these was the *Excelsior Orchestra* formed in 1914. It was in this context of local melodies, like the Osibisaba and Ashiko, being orchestrated for an upper-class audience, that the term "Highlife" was coined.

A third type of Highlife band was the low class guitar band which combined acoustic guitars with local hand drums, rattles and hand pianos. In the rural hinterland of southern Ghana and Sierra Leone, literally scores of these groups appeared, which played a less-Westernized Highlife than the posh urban bands. In Nigeria during the thirties a similar process occurred with guitar bands there playing a Yoruba music related to Highlife, called Juju music.

The Second World War and After

The War had a big impact on the dance band scene as Commonwealth and American troops stationed in West Africa brought in new musical ideas, particularly Swing. In fact, the first Swing band was set up in Accra by a British sax player, who called himself Sergeant Leopard. He employed both British army musicians and indigenous local players for his band, *Black and White Spots*. Unlike the huge prewar orchestras with their brass and strings,

Leopard's group started off a trend towards a smaller dance band consisting of trap drums, doublebass, guitar, and a front line of sax, trumpet, and trombone. A similar band formed by an English sax player and a Ghanaian pianist was the *Tempos*. These Swing bands played largely the army clubs and European clubs, but by the end of the war when the foreign troops had left, they had become Africanized. The most important was the *Tempos,* which by 1947 was completely composed of African musicians, and along with Swing and Ballroom music they started playing Highlifes. Their leader was E.T. Mensah and the drummer was Guy Warren, and between them they introduced a Latin percussion section of bongos, congas and maraccas, enlarging the band's repertoire to include Calypso — all the rage in West Africa during the fifties. This band thus became the prototype for the numerous postwar Highlife bands that sprang up throughout West Africa. For example, it was only after the *Tempos* had toured Nigeria in the early fifties that bands like Bobby Benson's, Victor Olaiya's, and Rex Lawson's started playing Highlifes. Consequently, E.T. Mensah became known as the "King of Highlife."

Meanwhile the acoustic guitar bands continued to grow in popularity. In Sierra Leone there was Kalenda's group, which played local Meringues and Highlifes. Less respectable were the various wandering groups like *Peter na Leopards* which played in low class beer bars and palm wine bars. In Nigeria Juju music kept gaining converts, especially after I.K. Dairo formed his *Blue Spots* band in 1957, though it was never played at the expensive hotels where only *Tempos* type bands were allowed. In Ghana the guitar bands increased in popularity, the most important being E.K. Nyame's, which in 1952 combined the separate traditions of guitar band Highlife and African comic theater (Concert). This theater originated in the coastal towns just after the First World War and spread rapidly through southern Ghana as it fused Western theater, and in particular, Vaudeville, with African characters and themes. The music that accompanied the acting was Ragtime, but E.K. Nyame replaced this with Highlife with such success that guitar bands and concerts are now inseparable.

One obvious feature, then, of both the dance bands and guitar bands has been their continual assimilation of foreign musical ideas and styles. The dance bands, which initially played ballroom numbers, Swing, and Highlife, have successively added to their repertoires Calypsos, Cha-Chas, Tangos, Congo music, and contemporary Pop music. The guitar bands have done likewise and their instrumentation has changed from an acoustic guitar band to a fully electrified one, with a P.A. system, electric guitars, trap drums, conga drums, rattles, and clips.

Black Musical Feedback

A striking feature in the development of Westernized African music is the influence of Black American music on it. As African musicians absorbed ideas from the West, they were more susceptible to this than the Classical music of the Europeans. The reason is not difficult to understand since Black music from both sides of the Atlantic is almost exclusively dance music and places great emphasis on rhythm. They have much in common.

Ragtime was one of the earliest Black American influences on Highlife and was introduced to Ghana in the 1920s through piano sheet music, by Afro-American seamen who congregated with their banjos in bars around the ports, and by the Vaudeville artists of the coastal towns. Other influences were the Foxtrots, Mambos and Rumbas of Black American origin played by high class groups like the *Accra Orchestra*. I have already mentioned the impact of Swing on the post-War dance bands, a music which has its roots in Jazz. Since then there has been a series of Black dance styles from the Caribbean and the Americas, culminating recently with Rock (i.e., R & B), Soul, and Reggae. A parallel feedback occurred with Congo music, a synthesis of African and Latin music that first appeared in Zaire about twenty-five years ago and then spread throughout francophone Africa. A present-day example is the Afro-beat explosion sparked off by Soul.

For many years, Jazz experts have traced the African heritage of Black American music, and lately have noted the increasing "Africanization" of Western Pop music (i.e. Jazz, R & B, Soul, Reggae, etc.: music that is indirectly African). Feedback is a third aspect of the cross-cultural musical exchange between Africa and the West and is a factor which is likely to lead to the *direct* impact of African music on Western Pop.

West African Pop Bands

By 1960, Rock and Roll was being played by both the guitar bands and *Tempos*-like dance bands. However, the first distinct pop band was the *Avengers*, formed in 1962 by a group of Ghanaian soldiers who had been affected by the music of Cliff Richard and Elvis Presley, while the Ghanaian soldiers were training in the U.K. Within a short time dozens of similar groups appeared, formed by school students and encouraged by promotors who organized "Pop Chains" (competitions) during the holidays. The next stage was the introduction of Soul, and the first West African band to play this was the *Heartbeats* of Sierra Leone, who, after a trip to Liberia in 1964, went into Ghana and Nigeria, spreading this music as they went. By the late 1960s, numerous Pop bands were playing Rock, Soul, and Underground music: such groups as the *Echoes* and *Akpata Jazz* of Sierra Leone, the *Saints,* the *Psychedelic Aliens* and the *El Pollos* of Ghana, the *Super Eagles* from Gambia, and the *Strangers,* the *Hykkers International* and Segun Bucknor's *Soul Assembly* from Nigeria. It is noteworthy that, except for an occasional Highlife and Congo number, they played "Copyright" music; that is, exact copies of Western Pop recordings.

The Change

There has been a dramatic change in the West African Pop scene since the '60s. The big dance bands have almost died out as the younger audiences think them too *colo* (colonial or square). On the other hand folk guitar music has become ever stronger. For example, in Ghana concert groups and guitar bands such as the *African Brothers, Wulomei,* and Konimo's are gaining popularity with even sophisticated urban audiences, a process encouraged by the government policy of cultural revival. In Nigeria, Juju music and Victor Uwaifo's "Benin sound" continue to claim converts, and in Sierra Leone they have "Milo Jazz," and updated local folk music.

At the same time, Pop bands have moved away from "Copyright" music towards a more creative and experimental attitude, with three main factors being catalytic: first and foremost is Afro-beat, a fusion of African music and Soul pioneered by Fela-Anikulapo (Ransome)

Kuti. He was first the leader of the *Koola Lobitos*, who tried to fuse Jazz and Highlife. After a trip to the United States in 1969, during which he "found his shortcomings," he returned, changed the band's name to the *Africa Seventy,* and concentrated exclusively on his Afrobeat. Many records have since followed his first release "Chop and Quench" (1970), and all the lyrics, which are in Yoruba or pidgin English, are tinged with controversy. "Shakara" (EMI 008N) is about sexual relations in modern Nigeria, and "Confusion" (EMI 0004) is about the hectic life in over-crowded Lagos. Another release, "Expensive Shit" (Sound Workshop Records), refers to a brush Fela-Anikulapo had with the police involving Indian hemp. "All Go Scatter" praises Nkrumah, Sekou Touré, and Amin, and "Zombie" criticizes the military mentality. His band, based at his club, the *Africa Shrine* in Lagos, consists of three guitarists, a trap drummer, and several conga, clips, and maracca players, with a front line of trumpets and saxes. Fela himself sings and plays electric piano or tenor sax and is accompanied by six female singers and a varying number of "Afro-sexy" dancers. He is one of the most popular musicians in West Africa.

Another factor encouraging Pop musicians to turn towards their own African music for inspiration is the Latin Rock of *Santana*. In 1971 this group played at the Soul to Soul concert in Accra, where their "Afro" sound subsequently encouraged a number of Ghanaian Pop bands to start using Latin and African drums. Then, of course, there is the important influence of the Ghanaian group *Osibisa,* which has visited West Africa several times since they came to fame in Britain.

The net result of these various influences has been the growth of many bands which combine African instruments like the drums, rattles, flutes, and xylophones, with electric guitars, to play a multitude of styles that go under the names of Afro-beat, Afro-Rock, Afrodelic Funk and so forth. From Ghana there are the *Big Beats, Boombaya,* and *Hedzolleh;* from Benin, the *Polyrhythmic Orchestra;* from Nigeria, *Mono-Mono, BLO, Ofege, Ofo,* and the *Funkees;* and from the Cameroons, *Manu Dibango.*

The simultaneous revival of folk music and the appearance of Afrobeat has also started to bring together the very separate traditions of the folk guitar bands and those bands influenced by Western Pop. For instance in Ghana, Ampadu, leader of the *African Brothers*, has brought out a synthesis of Highlife and Afro-beat which he calls Afro-hili. *Hedzolleh,* and sister bands like *Basa-Basa* and *Bunzu,* are basing many of their numbers on indigenous melodies, such as *Hedzolleh*'s number, "Rekpete," which is a rearrangement of an old Liberian sea shanty. Similarly, *Manu Dibango* has fused Soul with the traditional Cameroonian Highlife music called Makossa. In Nigeria, Sunny Ade has developed a style of Juju music influenced by Afro-beat, and Sonny Okosun has created Ozzidi music, a "Jungle Rock" based on Victor Uwaifo's style of music.

This brief survey will give, I hope, a clearer picture of the changes undergone by modern West African popular music, and it should be apparent that the African music of today is very different from that of the days when Highlife was evolving. During the early years of High-life development there was a colonial situation with the urban African musicians copying Western music, albeit largely Black American dance music. Today West Africa is independent. Local music is being given its rightful place and the Western music that is being assimilated is Black American music, which is in turn often looking towards Africa for inspiration.

In this collection of interviews and biographical sketches I have chosen some of the artists who have played a crucial role in the development of syncretic West African performing arts; that is, art forms that combine African and European elements in a qualitatively new style and in a manner relevant to the rapid social changes occuring in West Africa.

Chapters One through Four deal with four important Ghanaian artists, since Ghana is recognized as the birthplace of Highlife, the first of the syncretic dance music styles. In Chapter Five, on Simpa music, I look at the influence of Highlife on a purely indigenous music in order to show that Highlife not only has a dynamic relationship with the modern sector, but with traditional life as well.

In Chapters Six through Nine I turn to other areas in West Africa where syncretic music has developed. One very apparent feature that emerges is the great degree to which musicians of different areas have influenced one another; for instance, the diffusion of Highlife from Ghana, or the impact of Congo music on Highlife.

Chapter Ten is about Guy Warren (Kofi Ghanaba) who

anticipated many of the radical changes which have occurred in the West African music scene in the '60s and '70s. Chapters Eleven through Eighteen deal with the situation from the '60s to the present day, and Chapters Nineteen and Twenty are concerned with the musicians' unions and the recording industry.

In summary, those African musicians who previously had turned to Western music for guidance and inspiration are now coming to realize the wealth of their own African music. Moreover, many black American musicians are now working to embody the many distinct local sounds of West Africa in their new compositions and recordings. On both sides of the Atlantic, musicians are realizing the huge creative potential within the indigenous music of West Africa.

One

E.T. Mensah

Emmanuel Tetteh Mensah was born in 1919 in Ussher Town, known as "Old Accra," with its unpaved streets and thatched houses. He and his elder brother, Yebuah, probably both obtained their first interest in music from their father, a goldsmith and guitarist. Unfortunately they didn't stay often at their father's compound, but at their maternal grandmother's, in which lived a traditional fetish priest (a Wulomo). Their house, therefore, contained a shrine to one of the local gods, and the musical pair were often beaten by the Wulomo for breaking the taboo on singing and whistling around the house.

One after the other, the brothers entered the James Town Elementary School and, subsequently, its fife band, run by Teacher Lamptey, the Arts Master. In 1930 this famed footballer-come-bandmaster acquired a new string of instruments and, from among his flute- and piccolo-playing boys, formed the *Accra Orchestra,* an orchestra with a membership of about twenty-five. The instruments included cellos, violins, trumpets, saxophones, clarinets, guitars, and even a swannee whistle and musical saw. Although there were other bands around, such as the *Cape Coast Sugar Babies,* the *Winneba Orchestra* and *Sekondi Nanshamang,* it was the *Accra Orchestra* that was most renowned. All, however, played Waltzes, Quicksteps, Foxtrots, Ragtimes, Marches, Mambos, Rumbas, and Highlifes to their black elite audiences. Previously, Teacher Lamptey had been in one of the first dance orchestras in Ghana, the *Jazz Kings,* formed in the early 1920s and playing to the "High Society." It was probably in this context that the term "Highlife" was coined.

In the last century the West African coast was a virtual musical melting pot, and many styles, based on a fusion of indigenous music and that of sailors, missionaries and regimental fort bands, came and went. There were the Timo, Ashiko, Pati, Mainline, Gome and the most well known, the Fanti *Osibisaba*. So Highlife became the umbrella term for all these local styles orchestrated by the ballroom bands and brass bands.

After they left school, the two Mensah brothers, by then both playing the saxophone, formed the *Accra Rhythmic Orchestra,* which was similar to its predecessor minus the string section. However, the *Accra Orchestra* continued for many years, during which time many Ghanaian musicians, who later became famous, passed through.

The American and British troops, stationed in Ghana during the Second World War, had a marked effect on the dance band scene. The troops brought in Swing, and it is from this time that the night-clubs blossomed with such "exotic" American names as "Kalamazoo," "Weekend in Havana," and "The New York Bar." E.T. joined up with, and learned much from, a Scottish saxophone player, Sergeant Jack Leopard, who with his *Black and White Spots* toured around the army camps and European clubs. Later, just after the war, E.T. went on to join the *Tempos*, newly formed by an English engineer and sax player, Arthur Harriman, and a Ghanaian pianist, Adolf Doku. When these two left *Accra*, the group was reorganized by the Ga trumpeter, Joe Kelly; the drummer was the young Guy Warren. E.T. was also playing trumpet by this time.

In an interview with E.T. and Guy, I was told the story of how in 1948 they had to stop playing at the all-white European Club in Accra, originally their main spot. In the course of one of the dances there, a Canadian journalist racially insulted Guy, who had just come off stage for a break. Guy, in a furious temper, thrashed the man and the band was fired. Later the Canadian was asked to leave the country, for Guy was working as a journalist on one of the nationalist papers, and it was a delicate time for the British administration with the anti-colonial disturbances and lootings. The *Tempos* were offered the job back, if they agreed to find another drummer, but they turned it down, since Guy had introduced many new ideas to the group. He had played with Kenny Graham's *Afro-Cubists* in London and returned with Latin percussion instruments. He also came back with many Calypso tunes, all the rage in the Caribbean clubs there.

In 1950, Guy, Joe and most of the others split for Liberia and by 1951 E.T. had reorganized the band, this time as a full professional group, the first in the country. It was with this small (compared to the pre-war orchestras) band, with its front line composed of trumpet, trombone, and saxophones, that E.T. started making records for Decca. The rhythm section was composed of guitar, double bass, trap drums, congas, bongos, maraccas, and clips.

Throughout the '50s, this twelve man band travelled extensively around West Africa, especially Nigeria, which they first visited in 1950. E.T. recalls that when he first went there, the dance bands, such as Bobby Benson's and Sammy Akpabot's, were only playing ballroom music and Swing. Mensah's Latin/Swing style of Highlife became enormously popular in that country, and within a short time musicians there formed their own groups, modelled on the *Tempos*. The trumpeter, Victor Olaiya, split from Bobby Benson's band to form his own *Cool Cats*; similarly, Rex Lawson and Arinze left the *Empire Band* to start their own groups. In 1958 the *Tempos* made a grand tour of Africa, starting in Nigeria, then Sierra Leone, Guinea, and Liberia. They arrived in Conakry just a short time after the Guineans had voted for complete independence from France. In spite of the fact that the French had left unceremoniously, taking everything they could out of the country and destroying what they left behind, there were still trios of French musicians playing Cha-Chas, Boleros and Sambas at the nightclubs in the capital. E.T. and his boys were made especially welcome by the new President, Sekou Touré, since Ghana and Guinea had drawn very close politically.

An enormous number of musicians have been members of the *Tempos* since the 1950s, and many bands, such as the *Red Spots*, the *Rhythm Aces*, the *Star Rockets*, the *Planets*, and the *Tempos Graduates* which is now known as *"B" Soyaya*, started as break-aways from the group. By the time his band went to England in 1969, E.T. had two of his sons with him, on guitar and trumpet. As would be expected, there was some friction between them, for E.T. liked the Swing music approach, whereas the rest of the band, who were his sons' ages, wanted to play Congo music, Rock and Roll, and the Twist. E.T. was therefore forced to compromise, and the *Tempos* repertoire was enlarged yet again. In England they made an L.P. for Decca entitled "The King of African Highlife Rhythm," and they came back playing Reggae. Although it is now more a Pop group, with E.T. doubling on sax and trumpet, the band is still going strong. The *Tempos*, however, play an incredible range of music, from Waltzes and Highlifes right through to Dixieland and Soul.

E.T. Mensah (left) with Louis Armstrong during the All Stars Tour of Ghana in 1956

Two

Kwaa Mensah:
The Palm Wine Guitarist

In the introduction I mentioned the revival of guitar band Highlife that is occurring in Ghana at the moment. The Grand Old Man of this music is the Fanti musician Kwaa Mensah, who recently has decided to re-record some of his old numbers. He is the recognized master of the Palm Wine type of Highlife which, in contrast to the fully electrified guitar bands like *African Brothers,* utilizes acoustic guitar, giant bass hand piano, clips, and local hand drums. He therefore plays the most indigenous variety of Highlife. His uncle was the original "Sam," the first Highlife guitarist in Ghana. "Sam," or Kwame Asare, a goldsmith from Cape Coast, was taught the guitar by a Liberian seaman. In fact it was Sam who made one of the first Highlife releases when he went to England in 1928 to record for Zonophone.

Sam taught Kwaa the guitar, and during the '30s Kwaa played in a Cape Coast Adaha band, Adaha being a type of Highlife played on flutes, fifes, and brass band drums. Then in the '40s Kwaa joined up with a Konkoma group, a popular Highlife style of those days which specialized in complex drill-like dances performed in "fancy dress." Finally, in 1950, Kwaa formed his own guitar band and in 1952 cut his first single for H.M.V. At that time he received £5 cash for each number recorded, for royalties were then unheard of in Ghana. In 1955 Kwaa followed E.K. Nyame's example and added comic opera to his band's repertoire, with Kwaa playing the lady impersonator. He called his group *The Fanti Trio,* and it was so popular with the less-Westernized and more rural fans that by the early '60s he had released two hundred records.

For a long time, Kwaa's music was considered too "Bush" by more sophisticated Africans, especially by the young Pop fans who were surprised when they saw him at the Soul to Soul concert in Accra at Black Star Square in 1971. Some of the critics had thought that Kwaa's music was so old fashioned that he must be dead! Fortunately, with the new interest in old-style Highlife sparked off by *Wulomei's* success in 1972, Kwaa has made a comeback, even with the young. In 1975, Kwaa recorded an L.P. for Ambassador Records of Ghana and went on a month-and-a-half tour of the United States with *Wulomei.* He is currently preparing a series of L.P.s for Decca and is engaged in organizing a musicians' union.

The following is an edited transcript of an interview I had with Kwaa on 25 November, 1975, at Temple House in Jamestown, Accra.

Collins   Kwaa, you were born in Lagos in September, 1920 and brought up in Cape Coast. How did you first come to learn the guitar?

Mensah   When I reached Standard 5 my father and mother made some trouble so I had to leave my Cape Coast Elementary School just like that. I was a carpenter so I went to the Bubuaso mines near Dunkwa to find business, but I didn't get some so I went to the surveyor's department as a line-cutter [cutting lines through the bush for surveyors]. So when I was there I met one of my brother-in-law's nephews called Kofi Adzei. He was a guitarist and showed me how to play. That was in 1937. Then when my mother fetched me back to Cape Coast I met my uncle Sam, and he also taught me to play, and anywhere he goes I go with him. We were entertaining the soldiers during the war in Cape Coast, Kumasi and Accra. We made music and mime for the soldiers and army officers. I was the singer and clips player and he was playing guitar, singing and changing costumes. He used to dress up sometimes as a Sierra Leonese woman and sometimes as an Ashanti woman.

Collins   Tell me more about your Uncle Sam [who was born in 1903].

Mensah   Sam's father was a storekeeper who sold carpenters'
tools in Cape Coast. His father played the concertina and
used to take Sam, when he was very small, on his shoulders to play clips. His father played Adaha, the music of
the flute, fife and brass bands, and also Opim or Ohugua
[this is Akan Highlife played in three/four time with a
gong rhythm similar to Adaha, usually referred to today as
"Blues"]. Opim was special music for the concertina [i.e.
Blues played on this instrument]. Another rhythm they
played was Ashiko, a Highlife played with a musical saw.
Ashiko bands consisted of an accordian or concertina,
clips, and a carpenter's saw, where the saw is bent and
some iron or knife is used to rattle the mouth or face of
the saw. Sam later learned to play guitar against his
father's wishes, who thought only ruffians played guitar;
so Sam ran away to Kumasi and joined the *T.C.C. Company*. There in Kumasi he met Kwah Kanta from El Mina
and H.E. Biney from Cape Coast. Kwah Kanta played
wooden box and Biney and Sam played guitar. In 1928
they went to London to make recordings. Later, when
Biney died and Kanta left, Kwerku Bibi came in on guitar
and Kofi Lawyer on gong. Sam died about 1950.

Collins   Sam is usually considered to be your uncle, but this is not
actually correct, is it?

Mensah   No, Sam is in fact my *son*, but according to seniority I
treat him as uncle. You see, my mother's uncle married a
woman and had a child, and, as he is my mother's uncle's
son, he is my *son* [the Fantis are matrilineal, so Kwaa is
geneologically treating his matrikin as one unit]. Later my
mother's uncle and his wife divorced and the wife married another person and that man bore Sam. So Sam can
be called my *son* as he and the first child are brothers
from the same stomach.

Collins   Tell me more about your early musical activities.

Mensah   Before the war I was in an Adaha band called the *Atwem Band* [Atwem means drawing, as in drawing a bow], which consisted of a sidedrum which had a string at the back, pati drums, the angle [triangle], two pieces of iron, fifes and cymbals. I didn't use guitar in this band; I played pati and fifes. As a small boy I had played in the small boys' section of the *Atwem Band,* but when I returned to Cape Coast from the mines I joined the big one. In 1939 the *Silver Stars Konkoma Group* was formed, and I left the *Atwem Band.* When *Konkoma* came, it destroyed the *Atwem Band.* The *Konkoma* band had something like jazz drums, pati drums, bass, tenor and also tambourines [frame drums], and thirty singers. I was the first to bring guitar. We played Adaha music, Akan Adesim, which is a hot music faster than Highlife, Ashanti Blues, Rumbas, Foxtrots, Bumps-a-Daisy, Sambas, La Congas, Spanish music, and Dagomba Highlife.

Collins   What do you mean by Dagomba Highlife? Is it from the North?

Mensah   No, it was brought by the Kroos (from Liberia). The word possibly comes from a Kroo word, as one early Kroo Dagomba Highlife goes: *Dago mba wo ye tangebu.*

Collins   What happened after you joined the *Silver Stars*?

Mensah   I went on to form my own Akote special *Konkoma* group and I left when the war finished, as when the war finished, *Konkoma* finished. By this time I was a master guitarist and formed the *N.A.A.F.I. Franklin Band* and we played Highlifes, Ohugua...everything. *N.A.A.F.I.* means Navy, Army and Air Force Institute, and Franklin is a name I saw in the papers of a District Commissioner I went to see; I just liked the name. Then I formed the *Navy Blues,* which used apremprensemna [giant bass hand piano], pati, tambourines, cigarette pan and clips. The

Navy Blues collapsed when I went back to Kumasi in 1951, and when I came back after Christmas I formed Kwaa Mensah's band, which had the same instruments. My first recordings were with H.M.V. [His Master's Voice], and we were paid five pounds for each side. Altogether I've made nearly 200 records! At first I was not an actor, but the promoters forced me to be an actor, so I formed my concert party in 1955.

Collins   Kwaa, I am looking at the photograph, taken in 1959, of a scene from your play, "If You Bamboozle Somebody, He Will Bamboozle You." In this you are the good-time girl, Owurama, seated with guitar. The man with the black and white minstrel face and one leg thrown over yours is the joker, or *Bob,* of the play, the taxi-driver, Johnson. Behind you in top hat is the gentleman, Sousu, and behind Johnson with a pipe is the Old Lady. Could you tell me about the play?

Mensah   Johnson was a taxi driver, and because of the lifts he gave women he was always poor, so the owner took the taxi from him. Johnson had been taking cigarettes from some old lady's store to Owurama's shop, and bossed this old lady that, "I will marry you because I am a strong man so if anybody wants to buy cigarettes from you and they behave nonsense I will beat him." The old lady liked him and always gave him money and, as he liked to play the guitar, she went and bought guitar. The old lady didn't take the advice of the gentleman, Mr. Sousu, who wanted also to befriend her.

One day Owurama came to the shop to buy cigarettes and she met the old lady alone and saw the guitar lying down and asked her who gets the guitar. The old lady said she bought it for her man and gave it to Owurama to play. Then Johnson appeared and he was very happy, and he thought if he could get this woman he would like it. Owurama came again and Johnson told his wife to go and buy chop. Johnson told Owurama that he liked her but she said what about your wife. He said that she isn't my wife only an old lady he wants to help and the shop is for his own father. So then Owurama played the guitar and Johnson put his leg on hers. When the old lady came back, she met them like this. She said, "Hey, what are you doing here? So you be?" Then Mr. Sousu came and said to the old lady, "I told you I liked you but you said no, you like a young man." Then Johnson sacked the old lady and she took all the dresses she had given him so that only one remains and said to him, "What you have done me, someone will do you." Mr. Sousu hired suits to anyone that wanted them so Johnson hired a suit, to make fine play with Owurama. Owurama went away and came back to find Johnson in the beautiful suit and so she thought he had more money. She told him she had two brothers who had scholarships for overseas, so he gave her all his money. So when Mr. Sousu came he said, "Where's my money?" and took the suit. When Owurama returned she told Johnson that she wanted him to meet her mother so he should go and change his dirty old clothes. He told her that he had no suit so she abused him.

At the end of the play only Johnson is on stage and he says to the audience: "The first time I am a driver but I fall, then I saw some old lady and told her I would marry her and she agreed. But when I saw Owurama I went and called her and she took all my money; that's why I make like this. So if your wife is an old lady, or farmer, don't go and take the one with lipstick, otherwise you will fall."

Collins Kwaa, could you tell me about your future plans?

Mensah I don't want to make dialogue (plays) anymore, I want to make duet with the music. The musicians will speak and joke, then we will play and someone will dance, and afterwards one of us will say something again. I am going

Kwaa Mensah as a young man

Kwaa Mensah (with guitar) during a concert party in 1959

to continue my cultural music but I don't want to use any drum like a chief's drum or fetish drum. It's not good to play the Omanhene's (chief's) drum, and we are not fetish men. I am now making new long-playing records as some of my old numbers are very good and all the old records spoil.

Collins   To finish, what about some advice for young musicians?

Mensah   If you are a black man and you want to play Soul you can do it; you are white and you want to play cultural you can play. But if you mix them it is not good. My advice to young musicians is if you want to play culture, play real culture, and if you want to play Afro, play Afro. I am not advising them to stop, but if you are playing culture don't bring organ inside. But if you use guitar for cultural music it is fine. You see, the guitar came from Africa and the Europeans came to imitate it.

Three

The Concert Musician E.K. Nyame

After the Second World War, the folk guitar bands became popular, so that by the later '40s and early '50s there was a flourishing record market for their music, supplied by Akan groups (such as Appiah Adjekum's, Kwaa Mensah's, Otoo Larte's, Yebuah's, and E.K. Nyame's) and Ga groups (such as Obiba T.K.'s) which featured guitar and mandolin. Adjekum was an Akan resident in Accra, and his group's instruments consisted of bass, treble and tenor frame drums (known also as Gombe drums), finger gong gong, two acoustic guitars and an accordian. Kwaa Mensah, on the other hand, was based at Cape Coast, where in 1949 he formed a group similar to Adjekum's in composition, but also included an apremprensemna (bass hand piano). During these times the most popular Highlife styles with all these bands were the Akan Odonso (Blues), Konkoma, and the Ga Kolomashie.

The concert groups reflected a tradition quite different from the guitar bands, although both had spread throughout the Akan hinterland during the inter-war period. The posh coastal vaudeville concert gave way to trios that played to a less educated and more provincial audience. The most popular group was Bob Johnson's *Axim Trio*, and by the '40s a number of other groups had been created modelling themselves on it, such as the *Dix Covian Jokers*, the *Happy Trio*, the *West-end Trio*, the *Keta Trio*, the *Saltpond Trio,* the *Jovial Jokers* and the *Yanky Trio*. The music for these trios was supplied by a trap drummer and harmonium player, who travelled with the actors and played Quicksteps, Foxtrots, Waltzes, and Ragtimes.

However, today it is the guitar band that has become closely linked with concert, and the first to combine these two distinct art forms was E.K. Nyame, a Kwahu born in 1927. From 1948 this guitarist and singer was a member of Appiah Adjekum's band. Then in 1950, he left to form his own. Finally, in 1952, he formed a concert trio and merged it with his guitar band, naming the new group the *Akan Trio*. His synthesis of guitar band Highlife and Comic Opera was such a success that within a few years other guitar bands, for instance those of Kwaa Mensah, Onyina and Kakaiku, followed suit. Conversely, concerts already in existence enlarged their small musical section to a full-scale guitar band.

Below are fragments of a conversation I had with E.K. at his house in Jamestown, Accra on 25 May, 1975.

Collins   Tell me about the *Trio*'s early days.

Nyame   It was derived from the band, to give us our daily bread and let everyone know about the efforts we were making in our music. We staged in English, but there were parts of it when a character came in and spoke our dialect (Akan). But we minded the colonial ideology and British mind, so whatever we did in those days was in English. But by 1957 we were using Twi. We were the first concert to use guitar band and the first to use Spanish bongos, playing Highlifes, Ragtimes, and Calypsos in rare cases. I played the gentleman and Bob. The lady impersonator was Mr. Baidoo, and Okine was the lady in cloth or native attire; but Baidoo was in modern dress and hat.

We three introduced the show, but we had our own way: an opening chorus which was a Quickstep sung in English. In the early days we started the concert by eight-thirty, but gradually, later on, the time was increased to about ten or eleven o'clock. So between eight and eleven we would play records. The play would then last two hours; we were using Highlifes, Blues (Akan), and Christian songs.

Collins   You were originally with Appiah Adjekum's band. What was that like?

Nyame   I was a clerk at the time. It was an amateur group, and if anyone wanted to make some outdooring or function that needed music, we would go there. You know Appiah Adjekum is the originator of these modern (guitar) bands and the modern idea of music in Ghana. As for Sam (Kwame Asare), I can say it was folk music but not on the line of modernization. I played the fundamental (rhythm) guitar and Adjekum played the Hawaiian guitar. There were three oblong tambourines covered in vellum and about five to eight inches in size. The bass one was sat on. We also had a Four Corner (concertina) with 48 keys and castanets or claves. Sometimes Adjekum's wife played guitar.

Collins   Why did you leave Adjekum's band?

Nyame   I was having the idea of modernizing the music, to use staff notation and teach it in the modern way to raise the standard. At first we used tambourines, guitar and clips, but we made a change in 1951 and replaced the tambourines with bongos (treble), jazz drums (tenor) and fiddle bass (bass).

Collins   From where did you get the ideas for your stories? Could you describe one?

Nyame   When we create a very good Highlife number on the market, it's out of this we build our concert story, because the whole nation has the feeling that they want to see us performing what we have done on the recording side. We just narrate the story, then everybody will choose their part and just act. If you act well, we let you stay. If not, we fetch another person. We have so many plays that I can't mention (all of them). One we had was "Wo Sum Brodea

Sum Kwadu," which means "When You Push Plantain You Have to Push Banana" (i.e. you have to treat everyone equally). It is about when you have a child who does not come from your family you neglect the child and keep yours, not knowing that the child you neglected is rather to your interest and will come to your aid. It's just like these Lotto (lottery) numbers, you don't know which number is going to win. It (the play) is about a man who has married two wives and he loves another (more) than the other and the son of the one he rejected became a chief somewhere else. Then going on through some circumstances the son got to know the father had become poor and wretched, and so he brought the father up again.

Collins   You mentioned before that you sometimes used Christian music for your plays. So what is the difference between your concert and Cantata?

Nyame   With Cantata you have a complete cast, but in our trio there were only three people who did everything. Cantata is older than concert and many tribes do it (especially the Ewes). They use their own cultural music and combine it with Christian hymns. They always do these Christian doctrine and Bible stories, but we used modern stories.

Collins   Tell me about the time you went to Liberia and what it was like there.

Nyame   We went to Monrovia with the then Prime Minister, Kwame Nkrumah, for one week in 1953. When there was any function we would play for them at places like the Executive Mansion. They had no concerts there and no idea about them. What they did have was (Classical) music for piano and singer. We also met the *Regimental Police Band* which played wedding music, Swing, and any other type of music, provided the sheet was laid in front of them. This was the only time we travelled out of Ghana.

Collins   Since you first started recording in 1951, you have made about 400 singles for record companies like Decca, Queenophone, and H.M.V. What are some of your favorite numbers?

Nyame   One was "Menia Agya, Meni Na"("I Have No Father, No Mother"), which is about an orphan who is in trouble and nobody will come to his rescue. Another was "Mane Meoo Made Ye Mobo" ("Help Me As I Am Melancholic"), which is a plea to my ghost mother to help me from the grave. A very popular number was "Maye Maye Meni Aye" ("I Do Something Good and He Repays Me With Ingratitude"); even the Whites from the University liked it. One of our first popular numbers was "Onim Deefo Kukudurufu Kwame Nkrumah" ("Honorable Man and Hero Kwame Nkrumah"), which we did in 1950 to welcome Nkrumah out of prison.

Collins   At the moment you are busy with a series of L.P.s which you are going to release under the title of "Sankofa" ("Go Back and Retrieve"). These are recordings of your old numbers. Why are you doing this?

Nyame   Formerly our records were on the breakable 78s, and the songs are so good we want to leave them for the next generation, so any time they play our old songs they will become so much reflected back. You can't write this dance music, it's never written. I'm worried by this and this is why we are releasing our old numbers. If we don't, it will be something like a lost thing. Besides, the public kept telling me they want our old songs. Financially, we are not so much disturbed, but just to put the record down so that when we are dead and gone then they'll still be able to hear us. Highlife is important because all over West Africa Ghanaian Highlife is supreme. It's out of this that the Nigerians have their Afro-beat.

Collins   What are your other plans for the future?

Nyame   I intend to balance the whole musical trend and create a different sound that will suit the present epoch. Mine will be a developed Highlife, with changed rhythms, and I will use the Pati, which is like the tenor drum on a jazz drum and has a very high tune. I will use this Gombe idea instead of bass guitar. We changed over from bass fiddle to bass guitar in 1968. I will also use three tambourines, castanets and acoustic guitar. We will use a two-four beat; it will come near to Afro-beat.

Four

The Jaguar Jokers

The Jaguar Jokers is one of the longest established groups
performing in Ghana today. Mr. Bampoe, their leader, started his
acting career in 1946 at the age of eleven when he performed
Ananse and Bible stories in his elementary school plays. About the
same time, influenced by the *Axim Trio* who regularly lodged at his
home in Suhum, a town forty miles north of Accra, Bampoe and
some of his school friends formed the *Yanky Trio*. As Mr. Bampoe
describes it,* their families were initially not too happy about this:

> My senior uncle disagreed that a schoolboy should adopt this
> habit and we were told not to make concert again; but we
> were so stubborn you see. We used to go secretly and stage
> somewhere, and when we came home we would be beaten
> severely. This went on until after one holiday, after a longish
> tour, I showed him some sandals I had bought with the money
> I earned . . . This took my uncle by surprise and so he advised
> me that if I could make money out of the concert in my
> holidays, he had no objection.

After completing elementary school and a short period as a tailor
he joined the *City Trio,* and then in 1954 formed the *Jaguar Jokers.*
He used this name because:

> A jaguar is a wild animal—you can't make it laugh—but we
> can. In those days we had jaguar cars and to be "Jagwah"
> meant to be fine or modern. For instance a "Jagwah" man or
> woman was of high class.

---

*Bampoe's remarks are transcriptions of original taped interviews by the author.

A striking difference between the *Jaguar Jokers* and the earlier *Yanky Trio* and *City Trio* was that the former modelled itself on E.K.'s *Akan Trio* and, therefore, instead of hiring out Konkoma groups for the night, established their own guitar band which played Highlifes, Quicksteps, Foxtrots, Ragtimes, and Calypsos.

The *Jaguar Jokers* have reached an enormous audience in twenty years and besides extensive tours of Ghana and parts of the Ivory Coast, have made radio broadcasts since the late 1950s, and regularly appear on television today.

The group, composed of twenty musicians and actors, travels in a hired mini-bus and makes seven or eight major tours or "treks" a year, covering the whole of the country. Each trek begins on pay day (the end of the month), and lasts three weeks, during which time the band moves from town to town or village, playing every night. During the rainy season (May through August), they make a series of short local treks, with long periods of rest and rehearsal between, at their base town of Adoagyri, twenty miles north of Accra. The theaters used by the group vary from place to place and may be a cinema hall, a night club, or simply a private compound containing a crude wooden stage in the courtyard.

When the *Jaguar Jokers* arrive in a village or town some of the musicians campaign around the area in the mini-bus, making announcements, and playing music through a battery amplifier. Impact is heightened by large painted posters or cartoons, depicting scenes from the night's play, which hang from the sides of the bus.

The show itself starts at about nine in the evening with a dance in which the band plays a cross-section of current popular Ghanaian dance music. Below is a description of this dance or "inside rhythm," taken from Chapter Three of my book *The Jaguar Jokers: Comic Opera in Ghana.*

> Doku was on rhythm guitar, Jackson on bass, with Yaw Bob playing Highlife guitar and Ofei soul; they were supported by other members on trap drums, congas, maraccas, and claves. They started off with nine or ten Highlifes, Pachangas, Cha-cha-chas, and Congo numbers. One of the Highlifes was based on the Ewe Agbadja rhythm and another, the most popular (this was Christmas 1973), was a Nigerian one called "Oh Yea

Mama." After this it was time for "Souls," which included James Brown's "Gimme Some More," "Pop Corn," "Papa Got a Brand New Bag," and numbers such as "Funky," "Funky Four Corners," "Chain Gang," "Mr. Big Stuff," and one by Millicent Small. It also included some West African Soul, or Afro-beat as it is called: "Akula" (a Ghanaian number), several by Nigeria's Fela Ransome-Kuti, and "Music For Gong-Gong" by the London-based *Osibisa*. This last song was by far the most popular of all the songs that Christmas. The band also played Reggae, with Jimmy Cliff's "Synthetic World," "Grooving Out of Life," "It's Too Late," and "I Can See Clearly Now" the favorites. Other popular music was that of the *Staple Singers,* a band that came to fame in Ghana through the 1971 Soul to Soul concert at Black Star Square (in Accra). There was, of course, a "Smoochie-time" when the lights were dimmed and people danced to excruciating songs like "These Arms of Mine" and "All My Sorrows." The Souls finished on an Afro-beat number and were followed, after a fifteen minute break, by four Highlifes composed and sung by the newly arrived *Obeng,* songs which the *Jaguar Jokers* hopefully intend to have recorded.

The play starts when the theater is full, usually by eleven o'clock, and lasts three hours. After this the band plays again for a short while, the night's performances rarely finishing before two in the morning. The bandsmen sleep on the floor of the theater and are up early in the morning in order to travel to their next station.

The plays consist of an Opening and then a Scene, or play proper. The Opening was originally an hour long and, like the openings of the *Axim Trio,* consisted of a Chorus, In, and Duet,* in which the actors, with whitening around the mouth and eyes, tap-danced and sang Ragtimes. The Opening today is only twenty minutes in length, but still retains many features from the *Axim Trio,* including one of its

---

*The "Opening," "In," and "Duet" are the three parts of the beginning section of a concert party play. The "Opening" chorus is usually a Foxtrot or Quickstep, sung and danced by the principal actors. The "In" and "Duet" are both comedy sketches, the "In" performed by a single comedian and the "Duet" by two comic actors.

songs. It is within the Opening that the early Vaudeville influences have been retained.

The scenes, of which the *Jaguar Jokers* had fourteen in 1974, are each about three hours long, although in the group's early days they were shorter. Music for the plays is supplied by four of the musicians on drums and guitars. The plays are basically morality stories with a pronounced religious content (an influence from the Cantata format). They also contain many traditional features: they are performed in a local language; they employ indigenous music and dance; and they portray traditional figures such as chiefs, elders, and priests.

As with traditional Ghanaian performing arts, there is a great deal of audience participation, in the form of applauding, weeping, jeering, and throwing food or coins on stage. Sometimes spectators are so moved that they will go up to the stage with food and money, or stick coins on the moist foreheads of popular actors and musicians.

The characters in the plays are a cross-section of stereotypes found in Ghana today, including rural ones like the illiterate farmer and village elder and urban ones such as doctors, lawyers, and teachers. The young urban literate is also depicted, wearing the latest stylish clothes and using contemporary urban slang. Some of the lady impersonators play the role of adventurous "High time" girls who leave their villages for the excitement of city life. Like most concert groups, the *Jaguar Jokers* never employ actresses, as they feel women would not fit in with the rough traveling life they lead. Different ethnic groups also appear: the northern policeman speaking a mixture of Hausa, Twi, and Pidgin English; Lagotians with strong Yoruba accents; and Accra market women speaking Ga. Mr. Bampoe always clowns around in the role of Opia, an Ananse- (spider-) like imp, dearly loved by the audience.

Below is a synopsis of one of their plays performed in December 1973.

"Awisia Yi Wo Ani" ("Orphan Don't Glance Enviously")

Mr. Johnson is a building contractor who works away from home most of the time. He has three children, one by his dead wife, and two by his domineering second wife, Comfort.

A poster from a *Jaguar Jokers'* play "Awisia yi wo ani"

The *Jaguar Jokers'* minibus ready for "campaign" with poster and portable amplifier

Whenever he is away, Comfort favors her own children, the arrogant King Sam and the "Hightime" daughter Dansowa, over the unfortunate and humble orphan, Kofi Antobam. Opia is brought to the house as a servant, but the wife Comfort feeds neither him nor Kofi. Finally she decides to remove Kofi altogether by sending an evil spirit to him, but he is saved by three angels singing apostolic hymns. Mr. Johnson is so disturbed by his wife's behavior that he sends Kofi to Kumasi to complete his education, out of harm's way. Some years pass, and while Dansowa and King Sam are wasting their lives in beer bars listening to Pop music, Kofi is working hard at school and is rewarded by passing the Common Entrance Exam. He becomes a postmaster, marries and travels home to introduce his wife to the family. He arrives to find King Sam harassed by women and expelled from school. Kofi's wife gives advice to girls about the way they should go about looking for husbands. The couple then distributes presents to everyone and promises to help King Sam continue his education, if he mends his ways. Mr. Johnson sings the closing Highlife, in which he points out the problems of having children by different wives, especially preferential treatment of children by their own mothers, and maltreatment by stepmothers. He also advises young people to respect their elders, and suggests that if they are not succeeding in life they should move on and try their luck somewhere else.

The entire play contains forty numbers of various styles, as follows:

Highlifes	29
Fanti Funeral Song	1
Quicksteps	2
Hymns	4
Rock and Roll	1
Congo number	1
Soul	2
Total	40

Five

Dagomba Simpa Music

Simpa music grew out of a combination of traditional Dagomba and Hausa music with Western and particularly Western-influenced African styles. Thus, whereas Highlife emerged as a result of the direct influence of Western music on African music, Simpa represents a secondary syncretic phenomenon, for it evolved out of a fusion of the indigenous music of Dagbon with syncretic music from the coast (i.e. Gombe and Highlife). This secondary aspect of acculturation is also found in the music of other ethnic groups in Ghana: for instance, Ewe Bor-bor, Akan Boscoe and Ga Kpanlogo, all of which are local "cultural" music styles, influenced by Highlife.

As we have already seen, Highlife spread from the coast into the hinterland through the medium of records, brass bands, and guitar bands. By the 1930s it had reached Dagbon where it was transformed into Simpa. A clue to this Southern root of Simpa is the name *Simpa* itself, for this is the local name for *Winneba,* one of the Fanti port towns in which Highlife was born.

Today there are scores of Simpa groups scattered around the Dagomba traditional area (in Northern Ghana). It is predominantly a recreational music, played for and by young people; sometimes, however, it is played at weddings, funerals, and outdoorings. In Yendi, the capital of the Dagomba state, there are twelve groups, the two most important being the *Wait and See* and *Real Unity Stars* Simpa groups. I watched performances of both these bands in April 1974, and in each case the show took place in an open space in the town, illuminated by kerosene lamps, started at about nine in the evening and ended at one in the morning. The bands consisted of six or seven young male musicians and a chorus of girls between the ages of ten

33

and sixteen. Fifty to one hundred spectators surrounded the bands, and some of the girls present danced together, "flesh to flesh." Below is a more detailed description of the two bands and their songs. I should add that the repertoires are larger than normally played, as I asked them to play as wide a selection as possible.

Wait and See Simpa Group

There were six musicians in the group playing:
1) A set of Tamale-made metal conga drums
2) Three square frame drums: a bass, second, and solo
3) A gong-gong
4) A metal rattle made from an empty tin can
5) Although not used that night, the group sometimes uses a Hausa Donno or pressure drum.

Accompanying the group were one male and two female singers. Below is a list of the songs played. The list is short as the group did not play long due to competition from another Simpa group that was playing that night.
1) A long period of warming up by the drummers playing traditional Dagomba drumming
2) An instrumental Highlife
3) A "Congo" number called "Sopato," by O.K. Jazz, in which the words were in Hausa
4) An instrumental number with no name, but based on the James Brown Soul beat. The girls danced Soul.
5) A traditional Dagomba dance sung in Dagbani. The name translates as "Shake Your Waist."

The Real Unity Stars Simpa Group

In this group there were seven musicians playing:
1) Metal congas
2) Two frame drums: a bass and a second
3) A set of Tamale-made trap drums (a snare and two side drums)
4) A gong-gong

5) Metal rattles

6) A trumpet played by the leader, Halaru Sayiba

The group was accompanied by an ever changing group of female singers. The band was formed by Halaru Sayiba in 1967 after he left the Yendi brass band. He is, therefore, much older than the other musicians. He told me that his Simpa group traveled extensively around Dagbon. Below is a list of the songs (all of which were danced to by the spectators):

1) "I Can't Stand It," a Soul number by James Brown; however, the words were sung in Dagbani and translate as "A Monkey Carries A Baby On Its Back."

2) "Hip City," a Soul number by the *Champs*. Sung in Dagbani, the title is translated as "Fufu Is More Delicious Than Kontonte."

3) "Nimpa Rebree," a Highlife sung in Akan.

4) A traditional Dagomba dance, the lyrics of which translate as "If I were a fish I would stay deep down in the water where nothing could harm me."

5) "Sava Omo," a *Congo* number sung in French.

6) A traditional Dagomba dance, the lyrics of which, when translated, mean, "If a man insults me and then buys something for me, it is a double insult."

7) "Let's Do The Twist," by Chubby Checker, but sung in Dagbani.

8) A Kpanlogo called "ABCD."

9) "Everybody Likes Saturday Night," an old Highlife sung in English.

I mentioned that Simpa appeared in the Dagomba traditional area during the inter-war period; it was in fact the third of three genres of syncretic recreational dance music that appeared during this time. The first was Gombe music, which was brought from Prang, in Brong-Ahafo (120 miles south of Yendi). According to Shani Abraham, who was one of the six Dagombas who introduced this music to Yendi, Gombe was being played in Brong-Ahafo by Hausas and Kotokoles, and they utilized the full set of frame drums from the small tambourines to the large bass drum. A second style that appeared about the same time was Amidziro music. This was played on large empty kerosene cans and local congas, and was introduced to Yendi by Hausas from Salaga (seventy miles south of Yendi). The word *amidziro* is the Ewe word for stranger. Simpa music, which first appeared in Yendi and then spread throughout Dagbon, was a local development comprised of the previous two imported styles.

Shani Abraham recalls that the name *Gombe* was changed to *Simpa* in the twelfth year of Na Abdallah's reign (1932), whereas Issaca-Bukari, who helped organize the first Simpa group, put the time in the early reign of Na Muhammad (1938-1948). Mr. Bukari pointed out to me that Simpa in its early days was greatly influenced by gramophone records, and besides traditional Dagomba music, the groups played Akan Highlifes and European Waltzes, Foxtrots, and Quicksteps. Other influences on Simpa were from the concert parties, the first to tour the Northern Region being the *Axim Trio* in 1936 (see *The Story of Bob Johnson,* by Efua Sutherland, Anawuo Educational Publications). Yet another influence was from the brass bands with their *Adaha* Highlifes, marches, and ballroom music. According to Halaru Sayibu, two brass bands were formed in Yendi during the 1950s, one of which lasted until 1965. More recently, Simpa groups have incorporated Western Pop music (heard on radio, gramophone, or played by touring Ghanaian Copyright bands) into their repertoires.

Simpa music is also relevant to social tensions found within Dagomba society. The music has always been associated with young people and is frowned upon by the older generation, who consider Simpa gatherings as improper for young people to frequent. This is reminiscent of the attitude of the older generation in the West towards Pop bands and Pop festivals.

Finally, Simpa music plays an active role in the process of social change, and has been affected by the divisions within Dagomba society that have emerged since independence. During the colonial times, the British administration "froze" the traditional political system of chiefly succession, in which the Royal Skin was rotated between the various royal families or houses. With independence, bottled-up tensions erupted in conflict between the Abdallah House, supported by the British, and the Andani House, suppressed by the British and linked with Nkrumah's Convention Peoples Party (CPP).

This political division came to a head in 1969 when the Busia government forcibly expelled the Andani Regent from the palace in Yendi and replaced him with an Abdallah Ya Na (chief). The Simpa groups took sides in the dispute and made up songs about the conflict that were considered so inflammatory that a six-month police ban was placed on their performances. Since then the Simpa groups have remained divided.

The "Wait and See" Simpa group from Yendi, Northern Ghana

Six

Sierra Leone

Sierra Leone has a long tradition of syncretic Creole music influenced by seamen from America and the Caribbean, and by returning ex-slaves. According to the native musician, Samuel Oju King, two early forms of Creole music that were in existence before the Second World War were Maringa and Palm Wine music. Maringa was a local music played on the Congama, a large hand piano with four "keys" made of hacksaw blades, hand drums and a small metal trumpet that produced only one note. It was sung in Creole, or a local tongue, and is similar to Caribbean Meringue. The Palm Wine music, or Ragtime as it was also called, was a low class music played around the bars in Freetown by people like "Useless Man" Foster and the seaman, Eku. They played guitar and were accompanied by percussionists on cigarette tins and bottles. Below are a few examples of some of the songs these early groups played:

> "King Jimmy"
> King Jimmy around the water side,
> Bonga fish (herring) you get them every day,
> So if you want to cook your bonga fish,
> You can take a walk to the water side,
> Give me occra bongo soup,
> Boborombo na so we de (that's how we are),
> Get your fish from down K. baby,
> Fufu ne de fitiyie occra soup.

> "A Song About a Lazy Woman"
> I cook fufu it turn to starch,
> I cook agidi (unsweetened blancmange) it turn to pap,

You just sit down like Cinderella,
Ee! mon ami, ee! mon ami.

"Trungayaise" ("Ruffian")
Me Papa say make I no come out,
Me Mama say make I de na house.
But me Paddy come we go Lumley beach,
Moto-car go broke my waist.
Trungayaise no good-o.
I follow me Paddy we go Lumley beach,
Moto-car go broke my waist.

"Sweetie Palm Wine"
I catch a bus to Lumley
I meet a nice conductor,
Five shillings he charged me,
Because of my education,
The boys and girls were laughin',
They say I am a drunkard,
Thank God I am a freeborn
And Freetown is my colony,
Anywhere I go sweetie palm wine de wait for me.

E.T. Mensah and the *Tempos* visited Sierra Leone in 1958, and below is Mensah's description of the music scene there at that time. (Note: Mensah's remarks are transcriptions of original taped interviews by the author.)

There were no dance halls in Sierra Leone, and at the clubs they danced to gramophone records. Highlife was there but not under that name. We didn't see any guitar bands, although we did meet one boy who was popular for his guitar playing. We did hear some local Highlife records sung in Pidgin English, with the vocalist backed by one guitar. We picked up some of these songs from the town and two of them we later recorded. One of them was about a river, and we called it "Volta," and the other was "Fire de Come" (a very old Creole song). Another thing we noticed during our stay there was a class distinction between personalities. The upper class consisted of lawyers and doctors who would not like to mix up with the working class. If we wanted this upper class to attend separate fees and provide two separate dance floors to accommodate the two classes of dance fans. They didn't like the free mixture, as it was in Ghana or Nigeria. So if we called a dance and charged 7/6d, the upper class would not like to come; they would prefer to pay £3 double.

The song about a river that E.T. Mensah mentions is a local one called "River Rockeal," and it goes:

Rockeal, Rockeal, river Rockeal,
Me no savvy swim, water de carry me go,
Rockeal, Rockeal, river Rockeal.

Mensah states that Highlife music was played in Sierra Leone, but was referred to as Maringa, a development of local Palm Wine music, influenced by the Meringue music of the Caribbean. One of the most popular exponents of this Maringa music in the 1950s was the Creole musician Ebeneezer Calenda, and below are comments made by Samuel Oju King concerning him:

Calenda originally played the Gombe drum (a giant bass frame drum) and later formed his band, which was a brass band with one Gombe drum, two frame drums, guitars, flutes, recorders, trumpets, and a sousaphone that you wrap around your body. By the time I quit Sierra Leone in 1967, he was a fairly old man and had stopped music and was made a producer on Radio Sierra Leone.

Other popular groups of this period were *Peter na Leopard* and *W.P.,* or *Waking Profit* (because they made money from wake-keepings). These bands had no brass instruments, but featured the musical saw, guitar, drums, and triangle. Like Calenda's group, they played at weddings, funerals, and picnics, and were considered to be more respectable than the Palm Wine groups. Below is an old Maringa song that *Peter na Leopard* used to sing; it is in praise of a bride's mother, and King says that his grandmother used to sing it:

"Yawho (Bride's) Mammy"
Yawho mammy hebe (heavy) so, ...(chorus)
Who that you give 'em to, ...(Peter)
I give 'em to that little boy tonight, ...(chorus)

Where de bottle, ...(Peter)
Bottle de na room. ....(chorus)

By 1960 Highlife dance bands appeared as explained below by King:

> Highlife was very popular, and we had a couple of groups that played this music. One was the *Ticklers*, which had saxes, trumpets, guitars and was rather like the *Ramblers* (a large Ghanaian dance band led by Jerry Hanson), and was patronized by middle-aged Sierra Leonians. The *Ticklers* played Highlifes, Latin numbers, and Meringues which were a bit more polished than Calenda's. We also had the female *Police Orchestra*, a big band with women vocalists, drummers, guitarists, sax, and trumpet players.

By 1960, Rock and Roll also started to appear in Sierra Leone through radio and records, and was absorbed into the repertoires of bands like the *Ticklers* and *Police Orchestra*. However, the first Pop group there was the *Heartbeats*, formed in 1961-1962 by the young Creole musician Geraldo Pino.

The *Heartbeats* were modelled on Western Pop bands with three electric guitars, organ, trap drums and vocals. Inspired by them were a number of other Pop groups formed in Freetown such as the *Echoes* (this was the band King was in, formed in 1964), the *Red Stars*, and the *Golden Strings*, all composed mostly of students. *Akpata Jazz*, featuring Congo and Pop music, was another band started at this time, financed by the Prime Minister, Sir Albert Margai. According to King, the early Pop influences were:

> Rock and Roll like Cliff Richard's "Devil Woman" and "Put on Your Dancing Shoes" and Elvis Presley's "Jailhouse Rock." The Beatles were also popular with their "Hard Day's Night." Also, there was Sam Cooke, Fats Domino's "Hello Josephine" and Chubby Checker's "Twist."

In 1964 the *Heartbeats* went to Monrovia for two years and returned to Sierra Leone, having learned to play Soul. Liberia was the first West African country where the records of James Brown, Ray Charles, Otis Redding, and Wilson Pickett became popular. The *Heartbeats* were the first West African Soul band, and they went to

Ghana in 1966 and then Nigeria in 1968, spreading this music as they traveled.

Another creative influence on the music scene in Sierra Leone in the mid-60s was the Yellow Diamond nightclub, owned by a group called the *Leone Stars*. King told me that it was

> ...formed by the break-up of two groups. At this time (1964) we had some visiting bands, one called the *Outer Space*, from Nigeria, and a Ghanaian band based at the Tijuana nightclub in Freetown. Both bands were in town when they broke up. There were a couple of people from the *Outer Space* who were very popular in Sierra Leone, for instance Sharp Mike, a Nigerian trumpet player who had been popular in Ghana during the days of the *Star Gazers*, and Eddie Ewa, a sax player. They had a couple of friends from the Ghanaian band such as Tetteh, a trumpeter; Archei, a drummer; and Nat, a guitarist. They all teamed up with a Sierra Leonese conga drummer to form the *Leone Stars*, obtained a loan, and renovated a vacant club formerly called the Swazark Club. Progressive music like Jazz and Pop was played at the Yellow Diamond, and on Saturday afternoons they had jam sessions featuring prominent musicians. For instance, there was a black American guitarist called Woodie, who was a diplomat; another was a Ghanaian drummer called Buddy Peep, who had been in the United States playing jazz drums and knew Guy Warren. I jammed there, we all jammed there.

Instigated by the musicians who congregated around the club, a twelve hour jam session was organized at the Juba Barracks, just outside Freetown, at which fourteen bands played. Most, like the *Echoes, Golden Strings, Super Combo, Ticklers,* and *Akpata Jazz* came from Sierra Leone (the *Heartbeats* had left by then); but there was also a band from the Congo, *Bembeya Jazz* from Guinea and the *Formulas* from Britain.

Many of the young musicians left Sierra Leone as they found the music scene there too quiet, and they wanted to assimilate new ideas. As I mentioned, the *Heartbeats* left the country and ended up in Nigeria where they finally split up in 1971. The founder of the group, Geraldo Pino, recruited some Ghanaian musicians (known as the

Plastic Jims) and took them to Kano, while the other members remained in Lagos, taking the name *Baranta*. The *Echoes* left for Ghana in 1967 where Maurice Williams, leader of *Akpata Jazz*, joined them. *Super Combo* is now residing in London. Nevertheless, Meringue is still popular in Sierra Leone and an updated version of the folkish Maringa music has become all the rage there, under the the name "Milo Jazz."

Seven

Nigerian Juju Music, Apala, and Guitar Bands

Juju music is a Yoruba guitar band music and is derived from the various Palm Wine styles that emerged in western Nigeria during the '30s. Like the word "Highlife," "Juju" is a generic term used to cover a whole range of antecedent neo-folk styles that were played at funerals, weddings, and outdoorings which honored notable individuals. The more important of these music styles found in Yorubaland were Gombe (or Goumbeh), Konkoma, and Ashiko; these were played on local conga drums, maraccas, clips, rasps, and the samba, a small rectangular frame drum or tambourine. It is quite likely that these three neo-folk musics were imported from Ghana as Gombe; Ashiko appeared there during the First World War and Konkoma during the 1930s. Indeed, both E.T. Mensah and Victor Olaiya have have mentioned the fact that the wave of dance band Highlife that struck Nigeria in the 1950s was preceeded by an equally popular wave of Konkoma Highlife, all stemming from Ghana.

The Tunde King, a Yoruba musician, who first started playing in the mid-1930s, is generally recognized as the originator and earliest exponent of Juju music by Nigerian musicians, although it would be more correct to consider him the musician who fused already existing styles, like Gombe, Konkoma, and Ashiko, and called the result "Juju" music. He played the mandolin while other members of his group played drums, maraccas, and the samba drum.

However, during this period there were other similar and parallel forms of music that went under different names: for example, "Denge," a street music played on samba and guitar, and "Kokoro" (sometimes called Samba or Juju), a one-man-band type of music utilizing the samba. Another style that appeared in the 1940s was

"Ayidigbo," which was played on local drums and thumb piano, and seems to have been particularly influenced by Ghanaian Konkoma. The most famous of the Ayidigbo musicians was Adeolu Akinsanyu, who later in the 1950s formed the *Rio Lindo Orchestra*.

During the 1940s, two important Juju music innovators appeared. One was Ojoge Daniels, who played ukelele and banjo. The other was the guitarist, Ayinde Bakare, who teamed up with Daniel Akinolu and J. Oje in 1938. By 1957 their band had grown to ten members and became known as the *Inner Circle Orchestra*. However, the musician who really popularized Juju music was I.K. Dairo, who formed his *Blue Spots* band in 1957, and since then has produced literally hundreds of records. After I.K. Dairo, whose music was noticeably influenced by Highlife, the next milestone was Ebeneezer Obey. He formed the *International Brothers* in 1964. Obey is the pioneer of modern Juju music, which is slow, drawn out, and like a very slow Highlife. A striking feature found generally in Juju bands is that, due to the incredibly long hours the bands have to perform at social functions, the musicians sit behind the amplifier while playing rather than standing in front of it, as is found in Highlife guitar bands.

During the Nigerian Civil War, Juju music received a big boost, as it replaced Highlife as the most popular band music in western Nigeria. The reason for this was that, with the crisis, Highlife musicians from eastern Nigeria who were residing in Lagos (such artists as E.C. Arinze, Rex Lawson, Charles Iwegbue and Zeal Onyia), left for the East or went abroad. Only the Yoruba Highlife musicians (Bobby Benson, Victor Olaiya and Roy Chicago) were left in Lagos. Roy Chicago's band collapsed in 1970 when his bandsmen were absorbed into the army. Since then Highlife has never recovered its popularity in western Nigeria, and so Juju music has become the music of the Yoruba people.

In November 1974, I interviewed Ebeneezer Obey at his home in Lagos. He told me that he was born in 1942 in the small village of Idogo, in the Egbado Division of the Western State. He played in his own band, and in 1954 joined the *Royal Mambo Orchestra*, leaving to join the *Guinea Mambo Orchestra* in 1958. From there he became a member of *Fatal Rolling Dollars* band and the *Federal Rhythm Brothers*, finally forming his own band in 1964. Originally the band was called the *International Brothers*, but later Obey changed the name to the *Inter-Reformers;* today they can be seen at the Miliki Spot, Obey's nightclub in Lagos. He went on to tell me that during his early days he was particularly influenced by I.K. Dairo, but considers his own style an improvement upon it.

The *Inter-Reformers* band consists of three guitars (lead, rhythm and bass), talking drum or dundun (a double ended pressure drum played with sticks), sekere (maraccas), agogo (clips), and a male (large) and female (small) conga drum which Obey calls Gombe drums.

The top part of the Gombe drum is a Westernized drum with screws to tighten the skin, but joined to and supported by a carved, hollow traditional drum. (See figure below.)

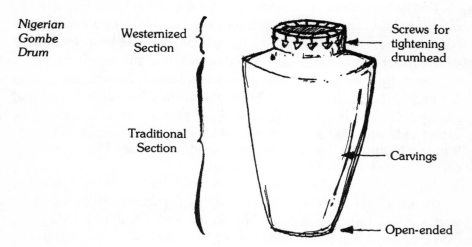

Nigerian Gombe Drum

Westernized Section

Screws for tightening drumhead

Traditional Section

Carvings

Open-ended

It is interesting to note that Gombe drums are found in Nigeria, Sierra Leone, and Ghana, although in the first case it is an indigenous hand-carved drum surmounted by a westernized drum, whereas in Ghana and Sierra Leone it is a large, bass frame drum. The musician sits on the frame drum and alters the tone by pressure from his heel which rests on the corner of the drum head. The drum head is tightened for playing by wooden wedges at the back, or sometimes a large metal screw. (See figure next page.)

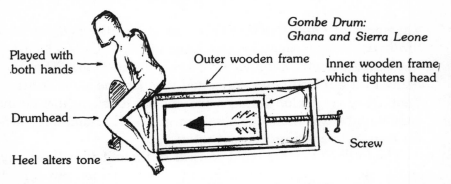

Gombe Drum:
Ghana and Sierra Leone

Played with both hands →

Drumhead →

Heel alters tone →

Outer wooden frame

Inner wooden frame which tightens head

Screw

The similarity between the Gombe drums from Nigeria and from Sierra Leone and Ghana is that both are local drums which incorporate western features. In the case of the Yoruba drum, a western side drum is carved out of an indigenous hand drum, whereas the drum from Ghana and Sierra Leone is using western techniques of carpentry and joinery.

Today Juju music is composed of a rather mixed bag. Many of the old-time Juju musicians are still playing, like I.K. Dairo and Daniel Akinolu who, since the death of Ayinde Bakare, has been the leader of the *Inner Circle Orchestra*. Ebeneezer Obey still reigns supreme, but recently two rivals have appeared: Idowu Animashaun, who formed his *Lisabi Brothers* in 1966 and plays Obey-style music, and Sunny Ade, who plays a more westernized type of Juju. The music of Sunny Ade and his *African Beats*, which he calls the *Syncro System*, is in fact influenced by Afro-beat and modern western Pop music and can be heard at his Q Club in Lagos.

Juju groups, therefore, now range from the traditional type to a modernized variety. *Sir Skiddo and his Mountain Millionaires*, a twelve man band based at Abeokuta, and Oladunni Oduguwa (Mummy Juju) and her *Decency and Unity Orchestra* are both bands that play the more traditional Juju music. *Prince Adekunle and his Western State Brothers* play a music which, according to my conversation with Segun Bucknor, is "Juju music combined with Afro-beat music." Other bands that play a music similar to Sunny Ade's mixed style are *Emperor Pick Peters*, *Thony Adex and his Sedico System*, and *Prince Dele Abiodun and his Top Hitters*. The latter played Highlife up to 1970, then changed to Juju Music and today plays an Afro-beat style of Juju known as the Adawa Sound. Bob Aledeniyi, originally second in command of the *African Beats*, split away from Sunny Ade in 1975 to form his *Jungle Rock Stars,* in which he is experimenting with Juju and Afro-beat. To facilitate this fusion he has recruited Segun Edo and Tutu Shorunme, former members of Fela's *Africa '70.* Thus Juju music is changing and absorbing new ideas, and it is not unusual today to hear a Juju number which utilizes a melody or refrain directly borrowed from western Pop music or Afro-beat.

Apala and Sakara

Apala and the related Sakara music are Moslem-influenced Yoruba music styles and like Juju music, they are mostly in the form of praise songs. There is some overlap with Juju music, as some Juju musicians, such as Idowu Animashaun, also play Apala. However, unlike Juju music, Apala and Sakara do not utilize European instruments at all; they use the dundun, one stringed or Gonje violin, and the sakara, a small round tambourine made of clay or bamboo and beaten with a stick.

Apala first appeared in the early 1940s under the names "Area" and "Oshugbo." Area was its name in Lagos, where is was played by musicians like Rashidi Oronla and Sekeri Performer. Oshugbo was the variety played by musicians such as Laisa Layema in Abeokuta and Tijani Ayanlolo in Ibadan. Haruna Ishola, the most famous Apala musician, formed his band in 1947. He changed the name Oshugbo to Apala and went on to make European tours and twenty-six long-playing records. Other popular Apala musicians today are Kasumu Adio, S.K.B. Ajao Oru (originally with Haruna Ishola), and Raji Uwonikoko with his *Kwara System,* the most recent addition being Ayinla Omowura (Baba Lonlo). The most popular Sakara musicians are Yusef Olatungii (Baba Legba) and S. Aka.

Midwest Guitar Bands

Juju music is not very popular in the Benin-Ishan area of the Midwest State, which boasts its own brand of Native Blues guitar bands. There is a tradition in this area of Palm Wine guitar bands dating from the Second World War. In fact, Victor Uwaifo was taught his craft by such guitarists. In this area today there are dozens of Native Blues guitar bands playing a music more similar to Highlife than Juju music and sung in the Edo language. The most famous, of course, is Victor Uwaifo, whose music is a very sophisticated and individual development of the local guitar band tradition. Several present-day leaders of other popular Blues bands have passed through Uwaifo's *Melody Maestros*, such as Collings Oke, who formed the *Odoligie Nobles,* Dandy Oboy, and Mudodo Osagie, who was with the *Melody Maestros* between 1965 and 1971, when he left to form the *Musketeers*, playing a Bini music he calls "Bushpower." Another musician who graduated from the *Melody Maestros* is Sonny Okosun, whose "Ozzidi" music is a mixture of Rock, Reggae and Uwaifo style music. Two popular musicians in the Midwest who, although never having been with Uwaifo, have been greatly influenced by him, are Aigbe Lebanty and Patrick Idahose.

Guitar Bands in Eastern Nigeria

Today Highlife is thriving in eastern Nigeria, with some of the most well-known guitar bands being the *Soundmakers,* the *Nkengas* (*ex-Soundmakers*), *Philosophers National,* Victor Chukwu's *Black Irokos,* the *Professional Seagulls,* the *Peacocks,* and Oliver de Coque.

The precursors of the guitar bands were the Palm Wine groups, and two of the most famous Palm Wine guitarists were Israel Nwaba and G.T. Owuka, who started playing before the Second World War. Israel Nwaba was from Aba and played hand piano and box guitar, accompanied by musicians playing bottles, clips, and local congas. G.T. Owuka also played box guitar and was accompanied by a rhythm tapped out on a cigarette tin. By the early 1950s, Highlife had made an appearance and was being played by guitar bands such as *Aderi Olariechi* from Owerri, *January* from Port Harcourt, and *Okonkwo Adigwe* from Asaba.

The Ghanaian influence on Nigerian guitar bands has been considerable, both on the Juju groups in the West and the Palm Wine groups in the Midwest and East. For instance, there was the effect of Ghanaian Konkoma in the 1930s, and in 1935 there was a tour of Nigeria by *The Cape Coast Sugar Babies Orchestra* and the *Axim*

Trio. In the 1950s E.K. Nyame was very popular in Nigeria, and it was also during this time that E.T. Mensah's *Tempos* made innumerable tours of Nigeria. Mensah's influence was very wide and affected Yoruba musicians such as Bobby Benson, Sammy Akpabot, Victor Olaiya and Roy Chicago, as well as Victor Uwaifo from the Midwest State and several musicians from Eastern Nigeria such as Rex Lawson, E.C. Arinze and Zeal Onyia. In fact, the trumpeter Zeal Onyia went to Ghana in 1953 and joined the *Tempos,* later going on to Spike Anyankor's *Rhythm Aces.*

During the 1950s and 1960s dance band and guitar band Highlife was the dominant music throughout Nigeria, and in addition to the Highlife musicians already mentioned, other popular ones were Charles Iwegbue and his *Archibogs,* Victor Chukwu, *Israel and the Three Night Wizards,* Eddie Okonta, Chief Billy Friday, Enyang Henshaw, King Kennytone, Onwuka, and Saint Augustine.

However, as I mentioned previously, Highlife lost much of its support in the West with the Nigerian crisis, its place being taken by Juju music. Nevertheless, Highlife has remained popular in Eastern Nigeria. Rex Lawson and his *River-men* was the most well-loved band, but with his recent death the band has continued as the *Professional Seagulls.* A band that has been greatly influenced by Rex Lawson is the *Peacocks,* formed in 1970 by Raphael Amaraebe, who had been a member of the *River-men.* The *Peacocks* is based at Owerri and today is influenced by Ghanaian Highlife musicians such as Akwaboah, Onyina, and K. Gyasi. The *Philosophers National* is led by Celestine Ukwu who was born in 1942, joined Michael Ejeagha's *Paradise Rhythm Orchestra* based at Enugu in 1962, and then formed his first band, *The Music Royals,* in Onitsha in 1966. A popular band in Aba is Paulson Kalu and his *Africana,* and in Owerri, the *Oriental Brothers* led by Godwin Kakaka. Stephen Osita Osadabe is the leader of *The Soundmakers.* Osadabe, born in 1936, joined Stephen Ameche's band in 1959, went on to the *Central Dance Band*, and finally formed *The Soundmakers* in 1964. In 1977, *Rokafil Jazz,* led by Prince Niko Mbarga, released their recording "Sweet Mother," which swept the whole of West Africa.

Haruna Ishola, a Nigerian
Apala musician

A poster describing a concert party given
by Francis Kenya and his *Riches Big Sound*

Eight

Music from the Congo and French-Speaking West Africa

Syncretic music only first surfaced in the French-speaking countries after the Second World War. By the early 1950s acculturated music, such as Mivenda Jean Bosco's guitar style of modernized Luba music, had come to prominence in Zaire. Bands mushroomed in the country during the decade, playing local music, sung in French or Lingala, heavily influenced by the Latin American music (particularly Rumbas) so popular throughout French-speaking Africa. This acculturated music became known as "Congo" music. Congo music rapidly spread to Francophone West Africa. E.T. Mensah remembers hearing it for the first time, played in 1957 by the *Melo Togos* in Togoland. By the late 1950s Congo records were also appearing in Ghana and Nigeria, and the first band to play them in Ghana was the *Shambros Band,* the resident band at the Lido Night Club, under the leadership of Ignace de Souza from the People's Republic of Benin (Dahomey).

E.T. Mensah's *Tempos* visited the French-speaking countries many times in the 1950s, and their comments on the situation are illuminating. They visited Guinea in 1958, when the most popular types of music at the time were the Cha-cha, Bolero, and Samba. They do not recall seeing any dance bands with African musicians, although they did see several European groups. In an interview, Dan Acquaye, a member of the *Tempos,* commented:

> We saw nightclubs with white musicians playing. You know, Guinea and these French West African states, they mix up with the whites. When a team from the Ivory Coast comes to play in Ghana you don't expect to see black footballers. No,

there is a mixture of black and white. When you go to Abidjan you don't expect to see blacks to be driving buses and taxis; the whites do the same. So we found white bands at the clubs in Conakry, playing French music.

The differences between the urban dance music of the English and French-speaking countries is amplified by E.T. Mensah's description of the *Tempos'* visit to Abidjan in 1955.*

The French were treating the country (Ivory Coast) as their own, you could see European taxi and bus drivers. In the markets were black and white butchers; the French had open shops side by side with the Africans. They did not leave the town to the blacks, so they brought the town up to date. They ran the night clubs and were importing European musicians and actors. We saw more of the whites in clubs than the blacks; the whites could afford the night club life. The white bands were playing Boleros, Cha-chas, Tangos and French music. When we played Highlife only a few of the Ghanaians there got up and danced, though by the end of the tour some of the whites began to catch on. When I went there in 1955 I never saw an African (dance) band.

He goes on to comment on the French territories in general:

The French dominated the blacks socially, and this affected the music, as the whites were doing everything. They had white musicians from Paris, but the African (dance band) musicians were not up to the standard so the (dance) music from the Africans was small. I should say though that in Guinea we did meet the leader of one African band, but even there we mostly saw white bands, usually small trios of say piano, violin and drums. The development socially and musically in the French territories has occurred since independence and they now want to catch up.

Similar comments are made by Ignace de Souza about the People's Republic of Benin.**

---

*E.T. Mensah's remarks are transcriptions of original taped interviews by the author.

**De Souza's remarks are transcriptions of original taped interviews by the author.

. . . (in 1955) we had an orchestra formed by the police and soldiers. But then you know it was the French who were ruling the country. They didn't encourage any (modern African) music . . . there were no guitar bands in Dahomey.

In fact, Ignace was a member of the first African dance band from that country. It was called *Alfa Jazz,* formed in 1953, which played Highlifes, Quicksteps, Boleros, and N'Goma music (Rumbas) from Zaire. It is also true that guitar bands (as opposed to dance bands) and concert parties were rare in the French-speaking areas. Although church-organized morality plays, or *Cantatas,* have long been popular in Togo, they have only had one Ewe concert party, formed in the 1960s and called the *Happy Stars.*

It would seem that during the colonial period in the French-speaking areas there was a pronounced demarcation between the indigenous "cultural" music on the one hand and urban music, dominated by the Europeans, on the other. However, in the English-speaking countries, African musicians were creatively experimenting with local and Western ideas by the turn of the century, resulting in Highlife in Ghana and Sierra Leone, Kroo guitar music in Liberia, and later in the 1930s, Juju music in Western Nigeria.

The present-day lineup of a Congo band is a Latin percussion section of trap drums, congas, bongos, clips, and maraccas; bass, rhythm, and lead electric guitars; and a front line of voices, saxophones, and trumpets. Zaire boasts literally scores of these bands with names such as *O.K. Jazz, L'Orchestre Negro Success, Orchestre Bella Bella, Orchestre Veve, Orchestre Bantu Jazz, Doudi Daniels and his Orchestra, Mando Negro,* and *Orchestre Congo '68.* The most famous singer in the country is Rochereau (now known as Tabule) who, by 1972, at the age of 32, had sold five million records.

With the influence of this music in French-speaking West Africa, many similar bands have appeared there since the late 1950s. The *Melo Togos* and *Eryko Jazz* were the first of such bands in Togo, who have since been joined by others such as *Orchestre Abass* and *La Voix d'Agou.* In the People's Republic of Benin there are *L'Orchestre Poly-Rhythmic de Cotonou,* the *Black Santiagos,* the *Jonas Pedro Dance Band,* and *Elrigo and his Los Commandos.* From the Ivory Coast comes the *Herikos International Dance Band* and from

Guinea *Bembeya Jazz*. A particularly famous singer from Togo was Bella Bellow, who, from the late 1960s until her untimely death in 1973, recorded many Highlifes, Agbadjas and Congo numbers in her native language, Ewe. She is also famous for her recording of "Rockia," the first Pop record in Ewe. Bella worked for a time in Paris with Manu Di Bango, another important French-speaking African musician. He is from the Cameroons and has been playing Congo music and Makossa music (local Cameroon Highlife) for many years with bands such as *Francois Lougah's Orchestra*. More recently he has been experimenting with fusions of indigenous Cameroonian music and Rhythm and Blues, and in 1972 he came up with a smash hit number in America called "Soul Makossa," released by the Makossa Record Company of New York. He is currently with Decca West Africa (the Afrodisia label).

Zairean music has also influenced English-speaking West Africa. It is widely heard in Eastern Nigeria and has influenced the Highlife there, even spreading down to South Africa and East Africa. In Kenya, for example, there are two very popular bands called *Gabriel Omollo and the Apollo Komesha '71* and *Super Mazembe*.

Congo music has been popular in Ghana since the early 1960s and is played by both dance bands and guitar bands. In Ghana, this music is usually referred to as *Kara-Kara*. A guitar band (and concert party) which specializes in this music is *Francis Kenya and his Riches Big Sound*. This band is made up of Nzimas and, as these people spread from Ghana into the Ivory Coast, all the band members can speak French. They play a Congo music with words in French or Nzima. To emphasize the popularity of this music in Ghana today, I should mention that the number one smash hit record in the country in 1976 was the Congo number "Shama-Shama," recorded by *Orchestre Cavache* from Zaire.

Nine

Ignace De Souza From The People's Republic of Benin

Ignace de Souza was born in the People's Republic of Benin in 1937 and was brought up in the capital city, Cotonu. He played trumpet and sax in the first professional dance band in that country, the *Alfa Jazz,* and later moved to Ghana where he first joined Spike Anyankor's *Rhythm Aces,* and then the *Shambros Band,* and finally, in 1964, forming his own group, the *Black Santiagos.* Ignace was the first musician to play Congo music in Ghana, where he stayed until 1970. He then returned to Cotonu and is now in Lagos with his band as the resident group at the Ritz Hotel.

I met Ignace in Benin City, Nigeria, during the latter part of 1975 when he was playing at Victor Uwaifo's Club 400 during the *Black Santiagos'* Christmas tour of the East and Midwest of Nigeria. Below is an edited transcript of an interview I had with Ignace on the 27th of December, 1975, in Benin City.

Collins How did you first become interested in music?

De Souza When I was young I learned music in the cultural way (i.e. traditional Fon music). From school I never liked music first of all, but after schooling I had a friend in Cotonu who kept forcing me to do music for two years. Then one morning in 1953 we went to the place that someone (a local man) had opened, as he was wanting to form a band. He had brought instruments and asked me what type I wanted to play. I saw many instruments, drums, saxophones, trombones, clarinets, and many others. There were two trumpets and I said I would like one because I saw only three valves and thought it would be simple to play. They laughed and gave me an alto sax and showed me how to play it and I gained it small small (little by little). The band was called *Alfa Jazz,* and the man told us after everything was going on we would be paid and would have a salary. We had a tenor player from Paris; he worked at the bank and every day he came in to teach us the theoretical part of the music and played with our group on Saturdays. Later on, the manager brought in two musicians from Nigeria: one was Baby-face Paul on tenor sax, and the other, Zeal Onyia, on trumpet. When Paul came he was pushing me on the sax, but when Zeal came I enjoyed the way he played better, so I switched to trumpet. So Zeal started teaching me the trumpet and I abandoned the sax. Since then I've concentrated on the trumpet. We played dance music, like Quicksteps, Highlifes and Boleros. At that time E.T. Mensah was reigning so we used to do some of his songs. It was a professional band and there were ten people in it.

Collins   Were there any other bands in the People's Republic at that time?

De Souza   In Dahomey we had an orchestra formed by the police and the soldiers. By then you know it was the French who were ruling the country and they didn't encourage any (dance band) music, only the military orchestras. E.T. Mensah and others used to play, as we had some night club owners who went to Ghana to bring them, but there were no guitar bands, although in some of the villages there were brass bands.

Collins   Why did you leave *Alfa Jazz?* And what did you do afterwards?

De Souza After everything was going nicely with the *Alfa Jazz*, the manager stopped paying us, so everybody had to find his way, and I chose to go to Ghana in 1955. There I joined a band called the *Rhythm Aces*. Zeal and Paul Babyface had left Cotonu to join the *Rhythm Aces* before me, but by the time I arrived they had left for Lagos. I played in the *Rhythm Aces* until 1956, when I went to the Lido night club (Accra), playing in a band called the *Shambros,* run by the Shahim Brothers, who were Lebanese. These Lebanese people were making a hell of a lot of money and at the end of every month they wouldn't pay us. All the time we were pocketless. I advised my musicians that we should make as one and start a bank account so that after one or two years we should have enough money to buy our own instruments, because these people were making fools out of us. The secret leaked out and they stopped me playing for three months, but when people saw my absence, the band didn't go too well because during those days the French music was making money. So the brothers brought me back and I told them that if they wanted me to work "number one," I would like to be paid more than the £9 a month I had been earning, and I would always like to have my pay at the end of the month; number two, as there was no day off I would like the band to have a rest every week on Mondays. So we signed the contract and I started getting £15 a month. I always kept £10 and saved it. Between 1954 and 1960 I started buying the instruments bit by bit. Then in 1961 I composed the Cha-cha number, "Paulina," and on the other side the Highlife number, "Patience is Best." The record became a hit and I used the *Shambros* in the recording but changed the name to the *Melody Aces.* I had the contract with Decca, and after the recording I paid the boys and kept what remained. I was lucky the record was a success and I made £700 in royalties, so I persuaded the man from Decca to sell me a set of instruments instead of paying me the money. So I bought two tenor saxophones, one alto, one trumpet, one guitar and I already had the drums and the other instruments. The man from Decca balanced me the rest, which was £350. I even bought materials for uniforms for whenever I would need it. I kept the instruments under my bed because I didn't want anyone to see them. Then by 1964 all my instruments were complete and I was finding a way for us to get out of the *Shambros* when there was trouble between the proprietor and the Minister of the Interior. The Lido was locked up and I had to run to the T.U.C. (Trade Union Council), where I made a report and we fought it out and they paid all that was due. Then I got a reasonable amount and went back to Cotonu and had my passport done. When I was there I thought of what sort of music I should introduce in Ghana, because at that time dance bands like the *Ramblers,* the *Armed Forces Band,* and the *Black Beats* were in top form. At that time there was nothing like *African Brothers* (i.e., electric guitar bands) and, in fact, Ampadu (leader of the *African Brothers*) was working under me during the Lido times—everyone used to come to me, as I taught the theoretical part of music. When I thought about which music to introduce, I knew that there was nothing like Congo music in Ghana, so I brought a bass player from Dahomey and went to Togoland to join with two boys who sang Congo music. I also brought many Congo records with me, and we learned them nicely in Accra. I formed the *Black Santiagos* and I made big posters, hand bills and radio announcements for our outdooring which was on the 11th of July, 1964 at the Metropole, where we played side by side with the *Ramblers.* That day there was a big turnout and many big men came, including some from the Dahomean Consulate, and I made almost £500 from the gate.

Collins   Did you travel much with the band?

De Souza   The band used to travel all over Ghana, but we didn't travel outside until Fela started coming to Ghana around 1968. He used to play at my place, the Ringway Hotel, which I had started to rent in 1965. Many bands played there. On Fridays the *Uhurus* or the *Ramblers* used to play and, when Geraldo Pino (of the *Heartbeats*) was around in 1967, I kept him and his boys at the Hotel and they used to play. When Fela became a good friend, he said to us that we should come to Nigeria for a few weeks, and we said we would if he would arrange it. In 1968 we played our first show with him at the Glover Memorial Hall in Lagos, and the next day we played at the Surulere Night Club (the original Africa Shrine), and there was a big turnout; after that we went to Lagos from time to time. During the Nigerian Civil War we toured all the Northern states and played at Cotonu and Lome on the way back to Ghana. We often used to play at Lome, as it is only 120 miles from Accra.

Collins   When did you leave Ghana?

De Souza   I left Ghana in 1970 because of the Aliens Order,* and I had to go as I was seeing my people being molested. Many of my musicians were Nigerians, and my organist was a professional Italian musician called Franco. So I went back to Cotonu. I was doing music there, but not like before; there it's not like Ghana where people patronize show business. There it's a bit boring.

Collins   What were the most popular bands in Cotonu and Lome ten years ago?

De Souza   In Dahomey we had the *Jonas Pedro Dance Band* and *Elrigo and his Los Commandos,* all playing Latin American rhythms and Congo music. In Togo there was

*The Aliens Compliance Order of 1969 was a policy of Dr. Busia, the leader of Ghana, which forced tens of thousands of non-Ghanaians to leave the country.

The Black Santiagos (Ignace De Souza is standing with trumpet)

Erico Jazz, the *Los Muchachos* and the *Melo Togo Dance Orchestra.*

Collins   And what about today?

De Souza   At the moment in Cotonu we have *Jonas Pedro, Elrigo*, the *Polyrhythmic Orchestra*, the *Les Astronauts, Disc Afrique* and my own band. In Lome things are a bit better because the type of politics our people are doing in Dahomey will not permit bands to do anything good. Musicians have to play from seven to eleven in the evening and then close up because of the curfew. At the moment in Lome there is the *Wilkomen Band* and bands at night clubs like the *Le Reve* and *Marquilla Noka*. The bands that play soul music have boys from Ghana; there are many Ghanaians in Togo.

Collins   What are the main differences in the dance music of the English and French-speaking countries?

De Souza   In the French countries right now they like Congo types of music, which is purely African, and they like a variety of music. Anything you play they will dance to. But here in the English-speaking countries they don't seem to like African music; they like Copyright and Soul, and others, which are not our fruit. In the French-speaking countries you can't keep on playing one way all the time, and if you play African music they like it.

Collins   Your band has Nigerian and Dahomean musicians and features a Senegalese singer on Congo numbers and a Ghanaian on Soul—pretty international. What are your plans?

De Souza   We are based in Cotonu, but we are now on tour of Nigeria (in fact the band has remained in Nigeria since this interview). In the East they like Highlife, but in the Midwest they don't; they like Funk and Soul. You know, in Nigeria Victor Uwaifo and the Juju bands are playing good African music. Fela has his own type of music, his arrangements are very good musically and theoretically, but I feel that it's still European because the background is jazzy, and Jazz is not our music. In Ghana they have many chances of improving African music better, but the musicians there just play Soul, Soul, Soul. If we don't take care, African music will be lost and our children will suffer. If we push the African music it will be good.

Ten

A Conversation with Kofi Ghanaba

I first met Kofi Ghanaba (formerly Guy Warren) when I went to his spacious house in Achimota with E.T. Mensah, in connection with the biography I was writing on E.T.'s famous *Tempos* dance band, of which Guy had been a member. Ghanaba, in Buddhist attire, talked to E.T. for several hours about their days together, and as we parted he invited me back for a second discussion, this time about the situation of modern Pop music. His remarks are transcriptions of my recorded interviews with him.

Guy was born in 1923, a member of the Akwei family of Accra. He was educated at Achimota College. Early in life he became interested in drums and was familiar with both traditional drum patterns and with Jazz drumming, and played at wartime bars catering to American and British servicemen in Accra. One of the first bands he joined was the *Accra Rhythmic Orchestra,* led by E.T.'s elder brother, Yebuah Mensah. This was a fifteen-member affair, formed in 1936 as an offshoot of the *Accra Orchestra,* and it played a cross-section of the current Ballroom music, Highlifes, and Ragtimes. In 1947 Guy was invited to join the recently formed *Tempos* band. As this was a seven-man group modelled on the Swing bands, it was much more to Guy's liking than the earlier colonial dance orchestras. E.T. recalls that whenever the *Tempos* played Waltzes, Foxtrots and Highlifes, Guy would play only half-heartedly, but as soon as it was a hot Jazz number he would play full belt. At that time Guy's eyes were fixed on America, and he developed a perfect American accent. In fact, many people thought he was a black American, which, as he explains below, caused him trouble at the Accra Club, a place the *Tempos* played at regularly.

During the intermission I went over to see a white guy who, like myself, was in publishing. This guy's Canadian friend said, "What's an American nigger doing here?" He thought I was an American and I thought he was one. He pushed me and I nearly saw red, as I had come to dislike the American whites intensely; by then I had been over there (he was in the United States for a few months before the Second World War) and had found all the propaganda about G.I.s being friendly a pile of horseshit. I thrashed his arse out. You see this was the sort of club where Africans were only seen padding about gently, dressed in white tunics, and here I came beating this guy up. It was a sensation. Just about the same time the C.P.P. (Convention Peoples Party) was forming, and I was the editor of a (nationalist) daily paper. So James (James Moxon of the Information Service) talked to me afterwards in my house, and he rushed to the Governor's Castle and told him that the Canadian must be sent away immediately, which he was (it being a delicate time for the British administration).

Guy flew to the U.K. shortly afterwards, where he joined up with Kenny Graham's *Afro-Cubists*, and returned to Ghana nine months later, bringing back many new ideas for the band.

When I came back from London I brought bongos and Cuban percussion to Ghana for the first time . . . Also when I was in London I went to the Caribbean Club, somewhere near Picadilly, the haunt of a lot of West Indians. It was all Calypso, every night, and I played these records on a B.B.C. program I had. When I came back I brought some of these records and we (the *Tempos*) learned to play them, as I knew straightaway that the musical inflections were so Highlife-ish.

The band only stayed together about a year after Guy's trip, and after a two week stay in Lagos in 1950, Guy and most of the other members of the *Tempos* split and left for Liberia. The reason for this was that E.T., who owned the instruments, wanted to create a synthesis of Highlife with Calypso and Latin American music, whereas Guy was more interested in fusing Jazz with Afro-Cuban drumming.

Guy stayed in Liberia for three years, working on a radio station, and just before he left he played at President Tubman's inauguration. From there Guy went to the United States, where he went even further with his musical experimentation of combining Black modern jazz with African drumming. It was in Chicago that he met his "muse," which, as he explains, was the realization that "I would be the African musician who reintroduced African music to America to get Americans to be aware of this cultural heritage of the black people." It was while he was in America during the 1950s that he produced a whole series of revolutionary L.P.s such as "Africa Speaks, Africa Answers," "Theme for African Drums," "Africa Sounds," and "Third Phase." Indeed, what Guy was doing then the present generation of Afro-beat musicians in West Africa have only just started to do. Guy is really their spiritual father and this is why he is constantly chiding the young musicians who only have eyes for Western Copyright music. Today the mature Kofi Ghanaba concentrates on indigenous African music.

The following interview is a condensed transcription of a conversation between Ghanaba and myself, recorded at his house on the 19th of August 1973. Some parts of the material have been edited and rearranged for the sake of continuity; otherwise it is verbatim.

Collins   African musicians have for a long time been assimilating Western music, and now whites are reciprocating. What do you think of the complicated relationship between white and black music?

Ghanaba   When I was in the States I couldn't work with any American bands because they wanted Afro-Cuban sounds and I wanted to play African rhythms. The black American is playing his version of African music, and then this version is being copied by the youth in the West. The reasons why this is happening so fast is because of the rapid communication system we now have.

Collins   One of the influences on the formation of Highlife itself has been black American music, from both North and South America.

Ghanaba   I call it bastardization.

Collins   Couldn't you just as well call it an enrichment?

Ghanaba   No, bastardization, because we came before them and the Afro-rhythms are derived from Africa. Afro-Americans were thinking that they would bring the African beat back home to teach to the people and it would become popular, like Jazz trumpets against an African background. I can't do that. I did that once, but now I don't consider this right, as I should have done it the other way around.

Collins   Could you mention some of the early musical influences on you?

Ghanaba   I've always been interested in traditional African music and Jazz, since my young days. We lived in downtown Accra, where they had this Gold Coast Bar (the Basshoun Bar) that catered to seamen, prostitutes and pimps. They had a combo there and every night they would play, and we would hear them from where we were (living). They played Ragtimes. I learned to tap dance. There was this great drummer who died, Harry Dodoo, a Jazz drummer and comedian who used to juggle with the sticks and joke around, just like a little Baby Dodds. Harry was my hero and I used to go to the bar and watch him play and dance. In the house where I lived there were some Ewe people, and every Saturday night they would hold a traditional drum session, for they are a very musical tribe . . . We also used to have masquerade parades in Accra every Christmas, and everybody would dance a sort of Poor Man's Quadrille to the sound of a bass drum, flute, and pati (small side-drum) . . . When I was young it was Jazz that dominated me. I was naive and thought that was the thing. But it is the African music that is the mother, not the other way around. I had to find this out the hard way.

Collins   Why did you change from playing Jazz to developing your own Afro-jazz fusions?

Ghanaba   It was a personal decision I made in my room in Chicago. I remember it very well. I said to myself, "Guy, you can never play like Gene Krupa, Max Roach or Louis Bellson. They have a different culture, and they can never play like you." I had to make a choice between being a poor imitation of Buddy Rich or playing something they couldn't. I could play Jazz well, but I possessed something that nobody else had, so I started to play African music with a little bit of Jazz thrown in, not Jazz with a little African thrown in.

Collins   The same thing seems to be happening to Afro-beat musicians today as happened to you twenty years ago. You have both been experimenting with mixing Black American and African music.

Ghanaba   That's very true.

Collins   It was even the same with Highlife to a certain extent. For even though it grew up in the colonial period it assimilated a lot from the dance orchestras and brass bands, with their black American Ragtimes and Rumbas. The big difference between the old Highlife days and today is that now, when Ghanaian musicians copy black American music, they have to turn to their own culture because this is where the most avant-garde Afro-American music is at, or moving towards.

Ghanaba   No, no, I don't think they can have it both ways—both of the worlds together like that! It's the education system here, it's still the same (i.e. colonial). There's been no revolution in Africa. These (Ghanaian) kids should realize that the last people they should imitate are people imitating them.

Collins   But surely it's a step in the right direction? The next step can only be a conscious turning by young Ghanaian Pop musicians towards their own traditional music?

Ghanaba   But musicians like my sons (Glen and Guy Warren, Jr.) are all the time influenced by Western newspapers, movies and television; and by commercialization.

Collins   But commercialization is not just a problem that faces West African musicians only.

Ghanaba   No, it affects the whole world. They always force things down the masses and the masses accept it, even if it's rubbish.

Collins   It's true that commercial interests usually trivialize music, but as soon as that happens a new layer of musicians turns up with a different sound altogether. Afro-beat, and the Afro-culture generally, may be partly a response to imported and commercialized "Afro" ideas from America, but, even so, it is a blow against the colonial mentality that is still so strong here in Ghana. You are getting a generation struggle through music.

Ghanaba   But this has been going on for a long time. The best that a black American can offer you musically, you dig; but it could never be like African music. So when Afro-Americans—Americans, I call them—tell us that we should be proud of our culture they are actually messing us up; because this (the imported "Afro" culture) is not our culture, it is theirs.

Collins   Western popular music has been greatly influenced by black music in America, and it looks as if it will soon be influenced by music coming directly from these shores; like Afro-beat.

Ghanaba   But the powers that be will never allow that to happen.

They will always compromise, as it is to their advantage to be flexible. If they ever tell you that you are succeeding (commercially), you are failing . . . I consider myself anonymous, my music is from the masses and I don't want it to have a commercial appeal. I have been a Jazz musician but now I am a Folk musician. In other words I have come home.

Since the time of this interview Ghanaba has put together the first volume of his autobiography. It is over a thousand pages, and the next volume promises to be of the same length. I helped proof-read the first volume in June 1975, and it made fascinating reading. When published, it will make an important contribution to the awareness and direction of modern African music.

Victor Uwaifo (with guitar) and author in the studio, recording the "Laugh and Cry" L.P.

Victor Uwaifo in concert

Eleven

Sir Victor Uwaifo

Victor Uwaifo was born in 1941 in Benin City, Nigeria, ancient capital of the Benin Empire. His primary and part of his secondary education took place there, and while at school Victor showed first signs of his talents as musician and artist. He made toy airplanes and cars, and even his first guitar. He was also an excellent sportsman, particularly good at track and field events and wrestling.

He completed his secondary education at the prestigious Saint Gregory's School in Lagos, where he continued his sporting and musical activities. He became the leader of the school band and in his spare time joined Victor Olaiya's dance band, the *All-Stars*.

In 1962 he won a scholarship to the Yaba College of Technology to study graphic arts, and divided his time into three main channels: studying in the morning, athletics in the afternoon, and playing music with E.C. Arinze's Highlife band at the Kakadu Club well into the night. All this he did on only four hours of sleep a day. After qualifying as a graphic artist he joined the Nigerian Television Service in 1964 and, while there, appeared on a weekly television program of Benin folk songs.

All this time Victor had been saving money for musical equipment; so that in 1965 he was able to form the *Melody Maestros*. In quick succession they brought out three singles on the Phonogram label called "Sirri, Sirri," "Joromi," and "Guitar Boy." It was "Joromi" that really made the band. Its lyrics were based on the tale of Gioromi, or "Joromi," a reckless wrestler, who against the wishes of his family decides he is good enough to take on the monsters in hell. The moral, sung in the chorus, is that discretion is the better part of valor. "Joromi" was so popular that it gave its name to the woven designs on West African shirts. Then, in 1969, Victor was awarded a gold disc by Phonogram for the sale of 100,000 copies of the record in West Africa—an unprecedented event. To top it all, he was "knighted" by the students of Nsukka University as "Sir Victor Uwaifo." Since then the *Melody Maestros* have released over one hundred singles and eight L.P.s on the Phonogram label. Below is a list of L.P.s up to 1976:

1) "Big Sounds," 1966
2) "Akwete," 1968
3) "Shadow," 1969
4) "Mutaba," 1969
5) "Ekassa," Volume 1, 1971
6) "Ekassa," Volume 2, 1973
7) "Ekassa," Volume 3, Sasakossa, 1974
8) "Ekassa," Volume 4, Sasakossa, 1975
9) "Laugh and Cry" [the only L.P. not on Phonogram], 1975
10) "Ekassa," Volume 5, Sasakossa, 1976

Victor Uwaifo's success led him and his musicians to visit many West African countries and in 1969 he represented Nigeria at the Black Arts Festival in Algeria where he won a bronze medal. Then in 1970 he toured the United States and played at Expo '70 in Japan. His most recent international tour was a grand tour in 1973 of Russia, Eastern Europe, and Western Europe.

In 1970 Victor moved from Lagos to his home town, Benin. Lagos was a "pot already overflowing," and he needed breathing space. In 1971 his Joromi Hotel, situated on the outskirts of Benin, was built, and this became his base.

I went to stay with Victor in the Christmas of 1975 at which time the Joromi Hotel, undergoing repairs, was temporarily closed down. Because of this, Victor had opened a new club right in the middle of town, Club 400, which, unlike the open-air Joromi Hotel, is an air-conditioned discotheque, complete with light show, stroboscopes and psychedelic posters. The club has a stage where the ten-man *Melody Maestros* play two or three times a week. One time when I was there Ignace de Souza, leader of the *Black Santiagos* from the Republic of Benin, played side by side with the *Melody Maestros,* with Ignace de Souza on trumpet and Victor on flute. Thus it was that Benin meets Benin.

Usually the show started with the *Melody Maestros* musicians warming up with "Souls" (Western Pop music), followed by the grand entrance of Victor, wearing spectacular self-designed clothes. From then on it was almost a one-man show, with Victor dancing, singing, playing Siamese guitar and waw-waw pedal, flute and electric organ. When playing the organ he would spin around or play it with his chin and make other "styles." Supporting the band were two midgets, and one of them, King Pago, who used to be with Bobby Benson in the fifties, danced with Victor, occasionally darting right between his legs, to the great amusement of the audience.

Below is an edited version of a series of interviews I had with Victor Uwaifo during the Christmas of 1975 in Benin.

Collins   Victor, could you tell me something about your family background and how it influenced your musical career.

Uwaifo   We were a family of thirteen and I was the last save for one. My father was a policeman and he rose to the rank of sergeant, which was very rare at that time; and when he retired he became a building contractor. He was a very strict and disciplined man; no wonder being a policeman. From when I was about two years old he used to call me to come and dance to Spanish tunes and Rumbas on gramophone records . . . I used to dance so well that it became an everyday thing. Whenever a stranger came, they would put on the gramophone for me to dance to and give me pennies. My whole family was musically inclined and everyone played one kind of instrument or another. My father used to play accordian and my mother was a very beautiful singer who used to take the lead in the church. All my other brothers grew up in that atmosphere and two of them are still musicians.

Collins   Tell me how you first learned to play the guitar as a schoolboy.

Uwaifo   During those days I used to go around to the palm-wine guitarists downtown. Each time they struck a chord it vibrated through my body and I thought I should be able to play that sort of thing too. The most famous of these guitarists in Benin was We-We, who had been a soldier during the Second World War. So I made a crude guitar myself, with high-tension wires for strings and bicycle spokes for the frets. But I started it all wrong, as I tuned the guitar to give me the So-Fa notation (i.e. tuned to a chord). I did this for almost a year trying a few songs, since I thought I was doing alright. Then one day I went to a palm-wine bar and borrowed a guitar to show off with; when to my amazement I couldn't play. I asked why I couldn't play it and tried to alter the tuning, but the man wouldn't allow me, as he told me his tuning was the correct and universal way. I didn't believe him and tried two other guitars, but they were the same. Finally I begged one of them to teach me to tune the guitar the proper way and he said not unless I brought him a jug of palm-wine. Fortunately I had sixpence on me, so I brought him a jug and he taught me to tune up and play some simple tunes. I took off from there.

Collins Although your father was a musician it seems that he was opposed to the guitar with its palm-wine connotations.

Uwaifo I found that my home-made guitar was very inferior, so I decided to buy one for myself. But it was difficult as I didn't know how to put it to my father, for he would never agree; the idea that I was going to buy a guitar would be a crime. So I decided to go somewhere and work to earn money as a laborer. Nearby they were building a new house and for seven days during the holidays I went there. I knew that my father, being so dignified, would be sad to hear that I needed to raise money in the same street; as if our family didn't have enough money. But I earned my one guinea and bought a second-hand guitar. The first time my father saw me playing it, he seized it and threatened to destroy it, but my mother saved it. She thought it would be better if she sold it and got the money back. I had to promise her that I would be a good boy and not bring the guitar back home and she gave it back.

Collins   Besides the palm-wine guitarists, who else helped you in your early musical development?

Uwaifo   I used to see E.T. Mensah and his *Tempos* play whenever they were in Benin, and the year I lost my father I went to see their guitarist Dizzy Acquaye, to put me through a few chords. I had a guitar book my brother had bought me but I didn't understand the chords; for instead of drawing the full neck of the guitar they only drew three frets. Dizzy helped me. Fortunately at Saint Gregory's we had a music tutor so I obtained a perfect knowledge of the rudiments of music. So I headed the school band. It was during these school days I spent nine months with Victor Olaiya's *All Stars,* playing during the holidays and weekends. But the school said I had to choose between them and the *All Stars;* so I had to leave Olaiya. It was during my time at Saint Gregory's that the whole revolution of school Pop bands started. The school band was formed to keep me within the gates and another was formed at King's College, Segun Bucknor being the leader. We used to have Saturday night out, either in our school or theirs, and we played Pop music like Cliff Richard and Elvis Presley, and also Highlifes of the E.T. variety . . . (later) I joined E.C. Arinze whose band was very versatile and played every kind of music. In those days you weren't recognized as a band leader unless you could play Waltzes, Quicksteps, Rumbas, Highlifes and everything. Musicians then were better, since it was like going through secondary school doing all subjects instead of majoring in one and having no knowledge of other subjects.

Collins   Every few years you seem to create a new sound. Could you tell me about these?

Uwaifo   All my early numbers belonged to my Akwete sound which I evolved by using colors to represent musical notes. It was at art school that I discovered colors in sound and sound in colors. I carried out some research in colors and was able to transpose them so that Do, the strongest note, was black; Re was red; Mi was blue; Fa was green; So, white, as it is a neutral color and sound; La, yellow; and Ti, violet. But the whole change came when I transposed the colors of Akwete cloth, hand-woven cloth made in Eastern Nigeria. It is a very beautiful cloth and you will see that different colors recur, creating a moving rhythm of color. When I interpreted this it gave the sound which I later called Akwete, and that was the beginning of "Joromi."

I concentrated on the Akwete rhythm from 1965 to 1968, but I got fed up with it because it didn't give me enough room to improvise. So I developed the Shadow, which was a link between the Akwete and the Twist. I first derived this dance as I stood one day and looked at my shadow and likened it to death—man's inevitable destiny. I thought that every movement in a dance casts a peculiar shadow on the ground. As the dance comes to an end the shadow cast by the movement of the dancer fades away, just as the body of a man perishes as he dies. To catch your own shadow is impossible, so out of this I created patterns and dance steps. The shadow lasted a year and I made an L.P. of it, but then Soul came and I started losing fans, so I had to bridge the gap. I had to create a rhythm similar to Soul as well as my original sound. This was Mutaba which lasted two years.

Then I came up with a new idea, Ekassa. In fact I wouldn't say I created Ekassa as it was already here as an indigenous dance of Benin. It was a royal dance done during the coronation of a new king and some people thought it an abomination to see Ekassa while the king was still alive. I didn't mind them as the first tune was a brilliant hit and others followed. Ekassa incorporates the beat of the tom-tom and agba drums, Western wind instruments, two guitars and, of course, me on the guitar singing in the Edo language.

After a few years I started to think of something else, in fact I'm always thinking of something new, so I created Sasakossa.

There was a time during the period when the Benin kingdom was overpowered by the British that the Benin massacre took place. It was when the King of England sent explorers to Africa to trade with the King of Benin. But the King had an important festival and said he would not grant the English an audience, but they were stubborn to come, and they were intercepted and killed. A few managed to escape to England where they were reinforced and came back for revenge. It was then that Benin was almost completely destroyed and the Oba (King) went into hiding. The King had an orderly named Sasakossa who used to sing in a popular way to warn him that there was danger and it was not safe to come out of hiding. He had a peculiar song he used to sing when it was safe to come out; the song was full of gimmicks. Whenever the white police got information about the hide-out they would track the King down, but the orderly or people around would warn him that enemies were around with the song. So that's where I got the rhythm for Sasakossa, my latest sound.

Collins Sometimes critics in the papers have suggested that your music is "Rock" or "Pop." What do you think of that?

Uwaifo Unfortunately, they fail to see that the foundation of my music is very cultural . . . my music is rich in African culture as demonstrated in the beat and lyrics. The fact that I use modern musical instruments to produce my sound has not altered the basic character of the music; otherwise we might as well argue that a historian writing ancient history with modern tools, like a Parker pen and paper, is a farce. The tools he uses to write his history will not alter the facts and the dates of his book. Nature abhors a vacuum. Thus we have experimentation and evolution of ancient African culture. My music is no exception to this natural phenomenon. It's the negative attitude of the press to expect me to produce what they want to hear. I produce what I have; otherwise I would be obliged to change my music from country to country. Since the beginning of my musical career my music has gone through stages (Akwete, Shadow, etc.) and all these stages have retained their cultural background.

Collins   You have been running the *Melody Maestros* for over ten years now. What are the main problems you have had as band leader?

Uwaifo   I suppose it's the same the whole world over. Here in Nigeria over fifty players have passed through me. It's not that I can't tolerate them, but after a time they become stagnant or uncontrollable. Or they don't find it interesting anymore to play with me as they want to branch out and find better opportunities elsewhere. Sometimes half the group has gone at one time and I have had to train the other half. Sometimes I have to dissolve the band because I don't find them useful anymore and can't work with them anymore. It's a task to keep the sound going.

Collins   That means that many present-day band leaders originally came out of your band.

Uwaifo   Yes, in fact one of the most recent is Sonny Okosun with his Ozzidi sound. He was a very good guitarist and didn't give me any trouble and I took him on a world tour once or twice. There are also other local ones like Dandy Oboy and Collings Oke, but it's a difficult thing to keep a band, especially since the new salary structure came in for the Nigerian Civil Service. After that everyone thought it was a right to review his or her salary, no matter whether in the private or public sector. It therefore affected small businesses and bands as well. I found that I had to pay almost twice as much as before and I didn't want to increase the charge at the gate.

I used to pay the band weekly but some of them do not live responsible lives, so I changed it to fortnightly; this didn't work as I found that some of them just worked for a fortnight, earned their salary and then you wouldn't see them again. So I changed it to a month, and now they have to give a month's notice. Another problem is musical instruments. You may lose one or two instruments at an engagement and it may cost you twice the money from the engagement to replace or repair them. It's especially hard for an artist who's made it to keep his standards.

Collins Your Joromi Hotel has been a great commercial success for you, but tell me some of your ideas concerning it.

Uwaifo Beyond the profit motive my intention is to use it to project African culture and progress. The place may be described as a museum, with its walls sprayed with artworks, including Benin carvings and paintings. These are designed to focus attention on the cultural heritage of the African people and their brothers who were thrown out of the continent by the waves of history. The hotel also provides, at a non-commercial rate, time for meetings on education and other programs calculated to foster the smooth sailing on the African yacht of peace and economic advancement.

Collins So besides being a musician, artist, and sportsman, it would seem that you consider the role of philanthropist as important?

Uwaifo Yes. Music is my means of livelihood and naturally one would expect that I only pull out the guitar where the quest is money—but this is not true of me. I often give free shows and donations in aid of the suffering and towards the advancement of human culture. For instance, I've played at many schools and colleges, health organizations and institutions for the blind.

Collins   It seems that similar altruistic ideals went into the design and plans of your residence?

Uwaifo   Yes, I put up my house as a lasting monument to posterity. I've seen things in England and Russia where writers' and poets' houses have been preserved. As long as I live I will live here, but even if I die, my fans will continue and this would be a monument where they could come and see how their idol lived. So none of my children are going to inherit this house as it's going to be a sort of tourist center and will be used to encourage young artists.

Twelve

The Dance Band Musician Stan Plange

Stan Plange is an Accra-born musician who has been playing guitar in dance bands for the last twenty years. In the late fifties, he was with the *Downbeats, Comets,* and *Stargazers,* and was treasurer of the Nigerian Union of Musicians between 1958 and 1961. In 1961, he joined the *Broadway Band* which was renamed *Uhurus* in 1964. He became leader of the *Uhurus* in 1965 and traveled with them abroad several times and arranged their music and recordings. He left the *Uhurus* in 1972 to lead the *Black Star Line* dance band. Then in 1973, he teamed up with Faisal Helwani of "F" Promotions to launch the Obibini record company and help produce records for *Hedzolleh, Basa-Basa,* and *Bunzu.* The following is an edited transcript of an interview I had with Stan Plange at the Napoleon Club on the 15th of February, 1977.

Collins   Could you tell me something about your early life?

Plange   I was born in Accra in April 1937 and, although I am a Ga, my family originally came from El Mina. I was in the school choir in elementary school at Achimota, but I wouldn't say this was the reason I became interested in music, as I tried to run away when there was singing practice. Our singing master claimed that I was a good tenor singer, so anytime I wasn't in, he noticed. Later, I did music when I was attending secondary school at the Ghana College in Winneba.

83

Collins You say you didn't like music at school. What then encouraged you?

Plange One thing was my father who was a trumpet player in the old *Accra Orchestra* of Teacher Lamptey. More important was when I used to see a group called the *Rhythm Aces* when we were staying near the Kit-Kat Club at Adabraka, opposite the Rodger Cinema. We used to go and stand outside behind the wall, and it was they who moved me to learn an instrument. Spike Anyankor was the leader, with Zeal Onyia and Baby-face Paul from Nigeria. Ray Ellis was on piano, Glen Cofie on trombone, Aggrey on guitar and Jimmy Wee Shall on double bass. They all came out of the *Tempos* except Freddy Tetteh (now with the *Continentals*) and Buddy Squire (now with the *Eden Church Band*) who came from the *Hotshots*. The *Rhythm Aces* came out with a unique sound compared to the *Tempos, Joe Kelly's* band, the *Red Spots*, and the *Hot Shots*. In those days, the *Rhythm Aces* were the best and had a big influence on me so I had to learn an instrument and forced myself into the *Downbeats*, although I couldn't play anything much.

Collins The *Downbeats* was your first band?

Plange Yes, I joined them in 1957, although I was practically playing nothing. I had left school by then and had worked with the Ghana Bank for a time. The *Downbeats* was led by Bill Friday—he's dead now—who graduated from Bobby Benson's band. He was an Ibo. I learned to play a bit of bass (fiddle) and congas and took up the bass. Unfortunately, two days before my first engagement at the Premier Hotel Akim Oda, Eddie Quansah came down from Kumasi to come and play. So, I lost the bass. Then, after we returned, Eddie said he was going to Kumasi to collect some things, but he never came back. So, I went back to the bass and played it for one year. Then our guitarist, Okyere, left. So, Oscar

More, who's now in London, came in. We had an engagement in Lome which was meant to be for the week-end. But after the promoter asked us to stay, Oscar said he had to go back to Ghana, so I had to take up the guitar. That year, we toured the whole of Togoland as at that time there were no bands in Togo and for all engagements, they used to get bands from Ghana here.

Collins   What happened when you returned?

Plange   I left the *Downbeats* and joined a new group that had been formed at the Tip-Toe. It was called the *Comets*, second band to the resident band, the *Rakers*. It was formed by Ray Ellis, our pianist and leader, myself on guitar, Prince Boeteng on trumpet (now with the *National Orchestra* and the *Continentals*), Lex King on alto sax, and Ad-lib Young Anim on trombone (he's now with the *Uhurus*), plus Tom Price on drums. Just three months after the band collapsed and we all thought Ray Ellis was to blame, the rest of us went to form a band called *Zenith*. It was financed by the Kwahu Union in Accra who had first formed the *Kwahu Union Orchestra*, led by Anima, but it had disintegrated and the instruments were left around—which we used. But after forming the *Zenith*, we wanted a leader since we didn't think we were ripe to lead a band. We saw Vanderpuie (he's now in London and has played with Eddie Quansah and Johnny Nash) but he wasn't ready to lead. We saw George Lee—the same! So, we were forced to go back and call Ray Ellis again. Then again, after three months, the band collapsed. Then all of us left for Kumasi to play at the Wilben Hotel and then went on to join the *Stargazers*. That was in 1958. The original leader was Glen Cofie but he left us and Eddie Quansah took over. The same year I left for Lagos to rejoin the *Downbeats* since Bill Friday had moved back to Lagos; so he sent for me and I stayed there until 1961. At first we played at a club called Nad's Club de Paris but the attendance wasn't good so we went to the Ambassador Hotel in Lagos for two and a half years. We played Highlifes and there were only four Nigerians in the group, the rest were Ghanaians. Later one of the Nigerians left and was replaced by the Ghanaian trombonist Pete Kwetey, now with the *Armed Forces Band*. When I was in Lagos I was also playing with the *Nigerian Broadcasting Orchestra* as guitarist and arranger.

Collins   Tell me more about what it was like in Nigeria.

Plange   The Nigerian music scene was very low. Except for the horn players, the Nigerian musicians weren't really good, the guitarists nil. Juju music wasn't recognized at that time. Nobody wanted to hear Juju, it was played in backyards. Highlife was the most popular music then and the most popular band was *E.C. Arinze and his Empire Orchestra*. In the *Downbeats*, I was the arranger and second leader, Joe Mensah was inside as a singer, George Emissah (who is now leading the *Uhurus*) on alto sax, Nat Hammond (or Lee Ampoumah) on bongos, and Akwei, who was nicknamed I Zero, on congas (he now plays alto sax for the *Black Star Line Band*). Joe Mensah and George Emissah went on leave and never returned, as they joined the *Broadway* dance band, run by the management of the Zenith Hotel in Takoradi and led by Sammy Obot. At that time, *Broadway* was being regarded as a national band in Ghana as it had been traveling with the late Kwame Nkrumah, and when Ghana Airways was being inaugurated, the band was going to Khartoum, Beirut, and so on. So, we began to think there were better opportunities back in Ghana rather than in Nigeria. Fortunately, the *Stargazers* band was being reformed by the present chairman of the Kumasi Youngsters Club and timber contractor, Collins Kusi, or D.K.C. as he is popularly known. He sent for me and I played under the leadership of Ad-lib Young. Then

from the *Stargazers*, I left to join the *Broadway* in
Takoradi around 1964 or 1965.

Collins   Up to that time had you done any recordings?

Plange   Yes, I made recordings with the *Stargazers*. I did the
arrangements. Then when I was in Lagos with the
Downbeats, we did a couple of recordings at Herbert
Ogunde's studio in Lagos, for Philips, with a group called
the *Harmonaires*. I arranged the band and we did two
singles that did very well; they were Highlifes with guitars,
drums, and vocals, but no horns.

Collins   How did the name *Broadway* get changed to the *Uhurus*
dance band?

Plange   What happened was that we came down to Accra on the
Arts Centre course in traditional drumming and dancing.
We stayed for three months and were housed at the
Puppet Theatre, near the Drama Studio. Our group,
George Lee's Messengers, and the *Farmers Council Band*
took advantage of the course. It was free for musicians.
When we returned, there was some trouble about our
salary so we decided that we would work with the
management on a percentage basis. But the percentage
they wanted was too much, taking into account the state
of the instruments, which were old. So, we left and within
two months we got E.K. Dadson and Krobo Eduse to buy
us instruments—in those days the whole set cost £1,600.
Later Dadson paid back Krobo Eduse his share, so the
band became Dadson's property. We continued to use
the name *Broadway*, as the manager of the Zenith hadn't
registered it; in fact, we registered. However, he took us
to court saying that the name belonged to him, and he
sued us for £2,000 each, or £26,000 for the thirteen of
us. He lost, but kept the name and was awarded £75
costs. So, we chose the name *Uhuru* (Swahili for
"freedom"). This was in 1964. Sammy Obot was leader

until 1965, when I took over. We went to Moscow for about six weeks when the Ghana Airways inaugurated its first flight to Moscow. In fact this was when we were still called *Broadway*, and we played on television, at Lumumba University and at the Metropole Hotel. We went together with Bob Cole, K. Gyasi, Onyina, and Sampson, the comedian. We made several tours of Nigeria. In 1966 or 1967, we went there on tour with Chubby Checker, went back to Ghana and returned just about when the Nigerian civil war was about to start. We left Nsukka when three days later the Biafran war started. We used to like the east best, as we had a lot of fans there and made a lot of money. The east was always the best market for Ghanaian music. In the late 60s, we made an L.P. for Philips and in 1970 made an L.P. for Decca in London. At that time, the band had three trumpets, three trombones and five saxes in the front line.

Collins   What about the East Africa trip you made in 1968?

Plange   Faisal Helwani was the promoter and the trip was sponsored by the East-Africa Airways. We were on the program together with the *Rolling Beats* dance-troupe led by Jackie Mensah, Guy Warren, and Willie Cheetham. When we were leaving, over half of my band didn't go. What happened was that the manager of the *Uhurus*, E.K. Dadson, said Faisal must pay half the money before going, but by the night before we were meant to leave he hadn't come to pay. So, by eight in the evening, Mr. Dadson told the secretary, who had most of our passports, to go home. So he left, thinking we wouldn't be traveling the following day, but after he left Faisal came to pay the amount and it didn't occur to Mr. Dadson that our passports were with his secretary. The following day, we were expecting this secretary to come to the airport with the rest of our passports. We waited and waited, so in the end, I rushed down to the office, but the secretary wasn't there. I finally managed to get the passports, but by the time I got back to the airport, the plane had gone with Faisal, the *Rolling Beats*, Willie Cheetham and four of my boys. Guy Warren didn't go either, even though Faisal sent someone to call him; he was annoyed or something. So me, 70% of my boys, and Guy Warren had to wait a week before going. We met up with the rest in Kampala where we played at a couple of nightclubs there and also on television. From there, we came down to Mombasa and then to Nairobi. We spent about five weeks in East Africa altogether.

Collins   Did you meet any musicians there?

Plange   Yes, we met one band from the Congo. In fact the local groups in East Africa play a type of Congo music sung in Swahili. They didn't play any Highlife.

Collins   You left the *Uhurus* in 1972. Why did you leave, and what happened afterwards?

Plange   I had trouble with the management. You see, what happened was that I was the artist and the repertoire representative for E.M.I. in Lagos. I got the *Uhurus* and *Hedzolleh* to record there. In fact, I was the first man to get a group from Ghana to the eight-track E.M.I. studio. I went back in 1972 to help in the re-mixing of the *Hedzolleh* and *Uhurus* recordings and, after I returned, there was some problem between myself and the *Uhuru* management and I had to resign. After this, I teamed up with Faisal to form a record company called Obibini Records. We decided we weren't going to give the *Hedzolleh* recordings to E.M.I. and we released two singles on our own label and intended to release an L.P. as well. After I had done the recordings I left with the tapes for Italy to negotiate for the songs to be on the sound-track of the film "Contact." Around this time Hugh Masekela came and, when I was in Italy, *Hedzolleh* and Hugh went to Nigeria to record the numbers again for the L.P. "Introducing *Hedzolleh*." Most of the titles on that recording were the same as the first recordings, but with Hugh Masekela on trumpet. After my association with Faisal, we couldn't go on due to financial problems, and I went to the *Black Star Line* as Musical Director of the band. I was there for nearly two years, and I left because I thought I was wasting my time there. After playing with private bands, I realized that the musicians in the government or corporation bands differed from the ones in private groups. In government and corporation bands, the musicians know at the end of every month they will get their salary whatever comes. So they don't care if they make mistakes or don't learn their assignments properly. In the private groups, you know that if you don't play well, or don't get any engagements, at the end of the month you'll be wondering where your salary is coming from. I tried to make changes in the bureaucracy of the *Black Star Line Band* but some of the musicians had been there 12 or 15 years; so in the end, I left.

Collins   Could you tell me about some of the recordings you did with the *Uhurus*?

Plange   I started doing experimental recordings with the *Uhurus*. My first was "Eno Brebre," which was all about advising a woman to be patient if she quarrels with her husband and not to wash her dirty linen in public. In those days, dance band musicians looked down on guitar band musicians as they thought they were an inferior type of musician. I tried to bring the two together and used dance band and guitar band musicians at the recording. From the guitar bands I used Frempong Manso as singer—he is now known as Osofo Dadzie. For the guitarist, I used S.K. Opong who is now the guitarist for the *Osofo Dadzie Concert Party*. (Osofo Dadzie is the most popular television concert show and specializes in plays about current social problems.) In fact, the reverse side of the record was Frempong Menso's composition and was called "Oh Mama Beka Akwantum" which said that if any trouble happens to a person the cause is bound to be another person. The other musicians were from the *Uhurus* dance band, like the vocalist Ed Ntreh, the drummer Rim Obeng, who's in the States now, and the Krobo singer Charlotte Dada, who was with the *Uhurus* at that time. Later on, we did two more recordings and in these we used the same vocal group plus Pat Thomas. The records were released on my own record label Nats Egnalp (Stan Plange backwards) Music Publishers.

Collins   What were your most successful recordings?

Plange   The ones I did with Opong and also another I composed with Joe Mensah called "Uhuru Special." But in fact, I didn't do so many compositions as arrangements.

Collins   *Uhurus* also used to play some Beebop, isn't that so?

Plange   The *Uhurus* itself played big-band jazz but a small group within the *Uhurus* was playing Beebop and appearing on television. It was called the *Bogarte Sounds*, with Ebow Dadson on tenor sax and Rim Obeng on drums. It was produced by this man who started *Osofo Dadzie*, Nana Bosompra. In fact it was I who introduced them to Nana. It was in 1969, and they started a television program called "Jatakrom" which later was called *Osofo Dadzie*.

Konimo

Thirteen

Konimo: A Ghanaian Folk Guitarist

I first met Konimo (Dan Amponsah) in 1973 at his home on the campus of the University of Science and Technology in Kumasi. I had been wanting to meet him for several years, since being bowled over by his music, which I had heard on a tape recorded by a friend of mine in 1970. His style of Highlife, which is based on the old Palm Wine playing that grew up in the Akan areas in the 1920s and 1930s, led me to expect an old guitarist, but the first thing that struck me about Dan was his youthful appearance. We played some music together, then I interviewed him, and then we arranged to meet the following week at the Philips recording studio in Kaneshie, where he and his group were going to record six singles. The seven man group consisted of Konimo on classical acoustic guitar; Little Noah, his twelve-year-old adopted son, on talking drums (Atumpan); and George Kusi and Yaw Nimo on the apremprensemna, a large variety of hand-piano on which the musician sits and supplies the bass line. Finally, there were Nyamekye, who played the long thin Gyama drum, and Bawauah, who furnished the gong patterns. On four of the numbers, I played the Asratoa, a small gourd rhythm instrument.

Below is a condensed transcription of an interview I had on August 1st, 1973, with Konimo, starting with his life story and ending up with some of his ideas and plans. I started off by asking him about his early musical experiences.

Konimo   I was born in 1934 at Fuase, eleven miles north of Kumasi, and my first experience with music was through my father who was a guitarist and trumpeter in the village brass band. One thing that was interesting about him was that he lost some of his fingers cutting cola nuts in a tree and was therefore similar to Django Reinhardt (a famous gypsy jazz guitarist, popular during World War II, who also lost some fingers). I started school there in 1939, and there was a chatechist called D.K. Sam who suggested to the Methodist community that they needed an organ. So I started lessons on this when I was five and when I was six or seven I was playing in chapel. In 1940, I went to live with my sister and her husband, Mr. Lawrence Osei Kwame Bonsu, brother of the King of the Asantehene. He sent me to the Presbyterian school in Kumasi where I was taught music. I was forced to spend hours listening to Bach and Beethoven as there were some German missionaries there who liked this sort of thing.

Collins   But why did they force you like this?

Konimo   The German missionaries were more militant. They detected something musical in me and felt they should help me.

Collins   What was their attitude like to traditional Ghanaian music?

Konimo   They weren't interested, except for Twi hymns; they were rather rigid. Music lessons were terrible for us in the school, although I did like the fantastic harmonies of the hymns and Bach type of music. Then I went to Adisadel College in Cape Coast from 1949 to 1952, and I was still playing organ. We also formed the *Adisadel* Highlife band, consisting of drums, guitar, and me on piano. I had a friend at the school called Harry Opoku, now a doctor, and one day I saw him playing an E.K. Nyame tune on the guitar; for at that time, E.K. was reigning. We were rivals and everything Harry could do I wanted to do better, so I picked up the guitar.

Collins   What happened after you left school?

Konimo   I taught in my village (Fuase) as a primary school teacher where I was the music master, so I organized groups of school children to perform some of Doctor Amu's songs on the radio. There was also a brass band in the village, so I learned to play the trombone, euphonium and tuba. I left there for the Medical Research Institute in Accra to do laboratory work, graduated in 1955 and went back to Kumasi where I started playing the guitar again and joined my first group called the *Antobre* group. We played Pop and Highlifes and used an amplifier: I was on guitar, Fred Aqufo was the alto singer, Ansong the treble singer, Yow Gyawu on congas, Kwese Kramo on bongos and, finally, Boakye on maraccas. This was a rival band to Onyina's which was then reigning in Kumasi; however, he did influence me very much. Then in 1957, I met the Head of Programs of Radio Ghana and joined a group of entertainers on a program called "Enne ye anigyea" ("Today is a happy day"). There were three of us: myself on guitar, T.G.B. Adjekum of Onyina's band as alto singer, and K. Qaino of E.K.'s band as first singer. About 1958 or 1959, I met Professor Laing, a pathologist, and I would say he has been my Godfather. He bought me a £60 Spanish guitar and I started lessons on the classical guitar, taught by Mr. Opoku Manwere. In 1960, I started working at the Chemistry Department of the University of Science and Technology and then got a scholarship to London to do further studies in chemistry techniques at the Paddington Technical College. While there, I entertained friends at private functions.

Collins   How did you get the name "Konimo"?

Konimo   The name means "Kofi who takes the blame for something he hasn't done." It was the name people gave to T.G.B. Adjekum, who was my uncle. We were only paid seven and sixpence per show and it was never regular due to red tape. So Adjekum left in 1958 and I took his name.

Collins   When did you make your first recordings?

Konimo   The first time ever was in May 1955, when I was at the Medical Research Institute in Accra. I got interested in I.E. Mason's band and recorded one song with them, a Dagomba number (a Highlife) called "Go Inside." My first recordings for the Ghana film industry were the "Driver's Lament" and "Owusu se Mamma" which I recorded with Doctor Kwame Gyasi in 1966. Then, in 1968, I met J.L. Latham from Salford University in the United Kingdom and he opened a fresh page of my life. He suggested that I translate my songs into English as many of the listeners at the private performances I gave were Europeans. These were translations of traditional ballads, some of which I have put to music and recorded (*Ashanti Ballads* by Konimo and J.L. Latham, published in 1969 by the authors). In 1969, I won a scholarship to Salford University to study laboratory techniques in bio-chemistry. But before I went, I met a friend called Van Spaal, a lecturer in engineering, and he recorded myself, Kwao-Sarfo on apremprensemna, and Bawuah on percussion. We sent the tapes to Mike Egan who was running the radio show "African Beat," and they were played on the B.B.C. External Service. When I was in Britain, I met Mike and made some more recordings for the B.B.C.—a program called "London Line." In 1970, I came back to Ghana and recorded four songs for Essiebons, with myself and Doctor Gyasi on guitars, Yow Nimo on apremprensemna—he's fantastic—and a donno (squeeze drum) player. The songs were "Farmers do farm," "Mammy where is my Daddy?," "I've worked in vain," and "Akosua give me a helping hand."

Collins   The music you play is a traditional sort of Highlife, the style developed by Sam (Kwame Asare) before the War and by Kwaa Mensah, E.K. Nyame, Appiah Adjekum, and Onyina after the War. Yet you have incorporated many foreign ideas; tell me about some of these influences.

Konimo   I find the classical musicians, the ones I was forced to listen to as a child at school—like Bach, Beethoven and Sibelius—tremendous. My Spanish influences are from Carulli, Carcassi, John Williams (whom I once met), and Julian Bream—especially his lute playing. I also like Dixieland and New Orleans Jazz and I saw Louis Armstrong when he came over to Kumasi (his second visit to Ghana in 1961). My two trips to the United Kingdom also helped. Kurt Anderson (Duke Ellington's first trumpeter) became a great friend of mine; I met Count Basie's guitarist, Freddie Green; I met Charlie Bird who influenced me a lot, and I met the prolific composer Jack Duarte who's got a wonderful record library. For guitar, my influences were Django Reinhardt, Charlie Christian, Wes Montgomery and Jim Hall. Professor Laing has also exposed me to Dizzy Gillespie, Thelonius Monk and Miles Davis. I also liked the oriental Indian music I saw in Manchester, especially the thing that was something like a calabash (the tabla drums). In Manchester, I got to know the Indian community, as I liked their peppers and used to practice yoga.

Collins   What about your attitude toward modern Afro-beat and Pop music?

Konimo   I like the beat but it's repetitive. I don't get the challenge since I hate boredom in music, and I think things should move. Some of the numbers also sound as if they are out of tune, and I hate this. Jimi Hendrix is often too loud, but I like his ambitious solo work. Reggae I like the best; it pulsates and pushes me. I prefer Bosanova to all this.

Collins   In spite of all these influences, your music is still like the old Palm Wine style.

Konimo   Yes, it is and in fact one woman told me that she thought my music was too "colo" (colonial or old-fashioned). Another person once remarked that when he first heard my music he thought I was an old illiterate running a store in a village. He thought I sounded like a "bush" man, somebody with no literary training at all. But I'm trying to experiment with the indigenous rhythms. You see, I don't like expensive instruments. I use the apremprensemna because it is cheap. I don't like amplifiers as I don't like to lay in large halls that need them. My music isn't really dance-music but is for listening to. I don't try to play pure traditional music as I like to move with the times and be experimental... for stagnant waters breed mosquitoes and this applies to music. I feel we should move but be guided by what we have, and feed this, like rivulets feed a stream.

Collins   Have you ever tried playing electric guitar?

Konimo   I've done a single recording on electric guitar. It was a record we did for the late Robert Mensah (a famous Ghanaian footballer killed in 1971). That was an experiment towards Bosanova.

Collins   The modern-day guitar bands and concerts are using electric guitars, rather than acoustic guitars and apremprensemna. What's your attitude to these bands?

Konimo   I don't like the way they are going for two reasons. Firstly, it is cheap music in the sense that the lyrics aren't well thought out; and also the language isn't decent. It should be sifted. There is some language the Akans won't tolerate, like "m'alomo" (a slang word for "my girlfriend"). It is necessary for musicians to sit down and think about balancing the lyrics and get the right thought. I don't like the use of common talk, for Akan music dwells on philosophy and the socially significant, whereas in European music love reigns supreme. Love is the thing, blah, blah, blah. In the Ghanaian songs that are concerned with love, some words should be given euphemisms. For example, in the Highlife song "Koforidua," about a young man who spells his own doom because he follows women and drink, people may think that when you go to Koforidua you are engulfed in this sort of thing. The second reason I don't like the modern guitar bands is that they are all monotonous. I like the *African Brothers*—I like the singer—sometimes I like the beat; but the accompaniment of guitars, and so on, is too monotonous. Also, although I like C.K. Mann's singing, his work is not true Osode and he is now waning, too commercialized. Listen to C.K. Mann and you will find it is all in E flat and F. Why is this so? It doesn't give any color. I know a story about an Indian who remarked to a Ghanaian audience in London who were enjoying the Highlife, "Kofi, do you only have one style of music?," because they were using the same harmonies all along.

Collins How do you think these problems can be overcome?

Konimo We all have to learn music seriously. I interviewed about forty people this morning for a band here in Kumasi and not a single one of them could read music. Well, Django Reinhardt couldn't read music, Wes Montgomery couldn't read music, but they were geniuses of their time, and if there is a legacy of written music from which you can draw, why not make use of it. Because, let's face it, we have been and are being exposed to western music. Now, if we want to sell Ghanaian music abroad we must get the thing well organized and you can't organize without getting the basics or rudiments. Jack Duarte wrote a guitar book and gave me a signed copy, saying that he hoped I was going to bring the classical guitar to Ghana. The inscription has always been at the back of my mind. I've decided to expose Ghanaians to the guitar and classical techniques. I want to set up a sort of institute here in Kumasi. In fact, I have been teaching the guitar since 1957 and one of my pupils who has come out is Mike Ofori, leader and guitarist of the *Dominos* Highlife band.

Collins What are your future plans in music?

Konimo From my corner I would like to develop percussion, then insert heavy chords into Highlife; rhythmic chords that will enrich the harmony. I'm going to marry the traditional Highlife guitar with Spanish and Latin-American music; an Afro-Spanish style using traditional rhythm with arpeggio—I always use finger picking, never the plectrum. Also, I want to develop an Afro-Jazz and use Wes Montgomery and Charlie Christian type chords in it. I'm thinking of bringing the European flute, and Durugya, which is an Akan horn played when the old chief dies. It has very low tones and is very melancholy. My interest at the present time is towards drumming and I've got a little boy whom I have adopted, called Little Noah, and he will be featured in our recording (of 11 August, 1973). I picked him up when he was nine and he's going to revolutionize my band; he plays the talking drums. At this recording I am going to use Kete rhythms (a traditional Akan music). The interesting thing about Kete is you sing, stop, then do drumming (call and response). I'm going to add the apremprensemna to provide us with the lower frequencies.

Fourteen

Wulomei and the Ghanaian Folk Revival

For some years now in Ghana there has been an accelerating awakening to the new folk music that arose as a result of contact with foreign musical influences. Highlife is the most widespread and well known of these and Konimo's guitar band from Kumasi is repopularizing the "Palm Wine" style pioneered by Sam (Kwame Asare) in the twenties. Similarly, C.K. Mann and his *Carousel Seven,* a band from Cape Coast, has been all the rage since they appeared with their raw Osode Highlife. Since E.K. Nyame linked the Highlife guitar band with comic acting in the mid-fifties, the resulting concert parties, and roving folk operas, have never looked back. Indeed, so popular have they become, that the Arts Council of Ghana organized a ten day festival for them in 1973, at which dozens of concerts staged and academics lectured.

This folk revival has been particularly apparent in and around Accra, where Ga bands like *Wulomei, Blemabii,* and *Abladei* have been catching everyone's attention with their Ga sea shanties, street songs, Pachangas, and a smattering of Akan Highlifes. The most important of these bands and the first to appear on the scene is *Wulomei* (the Ga word for "fetish priest"), founded by the Ga drummer Nii Ashitey.

On stage the members of *Wulomei* make an impressive sight with eleven Ga's, one Fanti, and one Ewe dressed in the white cloth of Wulomo (priest). The men wear frilly white caps and the three lady singers have their hair plaited like that of traditional priestesses. Nii Ashitey, the chief priest of the group, darts in and out of the musicians, directing them with staccato bursts on his long Osraman drum slung over his shoulder. The guitarist, a Fanti, sits well to the back of the stage with the rhythm section between him and the vocalists. The percussion instruments include congas, calabashes, a gong, clips, and a "tambourine." The latter is a square frame drum, also called a Gombe drum. They are of various sizes and on the largest sits the group's comedian, the beefy Nii Adu (Big Boy), who, by tapping the skin while altering its tension by pressure from his heel, produces a sound like a bass guitar. Around the microphones, melody is supplied by three female members singing the local songs in western harmony, supported by two male singers doubling up on the bamboo flute.

This band is not only popular with Ga's but with most Ghanaians, and its appeal seems to cross the boundaries between ethnic groups, generations and social strata. At one of their shows I recall being amazed by the variety of the audience: it included elite people in their "colo" suits and ties, young people in "Afro-gear," oversized market women carrying babies, and sedate elders in traditional cloth. The band's fame has been spread by records, especially their L.P. "Walatu Walasa," which they dedicated to the ideals of the government's self-reliance policy. When I asked Nii Ashitey what promted him to form the group, he replied, "To bring something out for the youth to progress and to forget foreign music and do their own thing." In fact, this is exactly what he has done: he has introduced local home-grown music to the present young generation of Pop fans, now receptive to "Afro" ideas.

Nii Ashitey started his musical career as a young boy just after the Second World War, when he played the Pati drum (a small side drum) in one of Accra's Konkoma groups, the *Navy Babies*. Later he became a conga player and joined a number of dance bands, including E.T. Mensah's *Tempos*. He spent some time in Liberia, as a member of the *Tubman Stars* dance band, and returned home to the *Police Band* and the *Brigade Band Number Two,* before forming *Wulomei*. He told me that *Wulomei* has incorporated material from various local sources, the most important being that of Obiba T.K., a Ga musician who led a Konkoma group in Accra in the forties. This group used tambourines (Gombe drums), mandolin, and guitar, and played Akan Highlifes and Ga Kolomashies. Another style that has affected *Wulomei* is the "Something" music popular with Ga fishermen in the fifties, played on guitar, bass, and lead hand piano. Also included in *Wulomei*'s repertoire is Oge, a music associated with the Liberian Kroo seamen who lived in Accra in the fifties, and Kpanlogo, a successor to Kolomashie and Oge. *Wulomei* even includes a few Dagbani songs from Northern Ghana and therefore presents a broad range of Ghanaian folk music to its audience.

The Gombe drums used by *Wulomei* and similar Ga groups have an interesting history that spans several West African countries. They were introduced to Ghana around the turn of the century by Ga artisans returning from working in the Cameroons. The Gombe rhythms played on these drums subsequently became associated with other urban folk styles such as the Ga Ashiko and Fanti Osibisaba, known collectively by the twenties as Highlife. Gombe drums are also found in Sierra Leone, where identical frame drums comprise part of the ensemble of the Meringue groups. According to Nigeria's Ebeneezer Obey, one of the drums found in Yoruba Juju guitar bands is the Gombe drum, in this case not a frame drum, but one in which the base, a traditional carved open-ended hand drum, is surmounted by a Western-type side drum, complete with metal screws for tightening the head. In all cases the common feature of the Gombe drum is that it is a local West African drum which possesses features borrowed from the West.

Wulomei's first L.P. was "Walatu Walasa," which they released in 1974. It includes numbers such as "Menye," "Soyama," and the very popular "Walatu Walasa" and "Akrowa" which they also released as singles. In March 1975, they signed a three year contract with Phonogram and the same year released a second L.P. called "*Wulomei* in Drum Conference." This record consisted of ten numbers, nine Ga songs and an old Liberian song that dates back to the forties. In June and July 1975, *Wulomei,* accompanied by the Kwaa Mensah group and the Gonje group of Salisu Mahama, made a forty-five day tour of America which began at the Festival of American Folklore held in Washington, D.C.

The Funkees, an Afro-beat band from Nigeria

Fifteen

Pop Music in West Africa

From about 1960, Rock and Roll, the Twist, and Pop music generally started becoming popular in West Africa. The very first Pop bands there were the *Avengers* from Ghana, the *Heartbeats* from Sierra Leone, and the *Blue Knights* from Nigeria. Since Pop music is sung in English, it predictably first caught on in English-speaking West African nations, and only later did it spread to the French-speaking areas. Even today many of the Pop musicians playing in countries such as Togo, Ivory Coast, Upper Volta and Senegal are from Ghana, Nigeria and Sierra Leone. I have already dealt with the Pop scene in Sierra Leone in Chapter Six, and I will here examine the the early Pop scene in Ghana and Nigeria.

As I mentioned, the first Pop band (as opposed to a Dance band playing Pop numbers) in Ghana was the *Avengers,* formed in 1962 from an army band called the *Red Devils.* Gabby Nick Valdo was the leader and he formed the *Avengers* after he and some of the members of the *Red Devils* had spent some time training in England, where they saw Pop groups such as Cliff Richard and the *Shadows.* The *Avengers* subsequently inspired a whole number of student Pop bands such as Ricky Telfer's *Bachelors* and the *Sharks,* based at the Achimota school. By 1966, Pop competitions, or "Pop Chains" as they were called, were being organized in Accra during the school holidays, with schoolboy bands such as the *Road Runners, Blues Syndicate, Circuit Five, Phantoms,* and the *Saints* jostling for first place, playing the music of Elvis Presley, the Beatles, the Rolling Stones and Spencer Davis. In 1966 the *Heartbeats* hit the country, introducing live Soul music. The first Ghanaian band to play this was the *El Pollos,* led by Stanley Todd and Elvis J. Brown. Even the Dance bands started playing Pop and Soul. Like King Bruce's old *Black Beats* which, under the youthful leadership of Sammy Owusu, hired the Soul singer Ray Otis. King Bruce also formed a new band called the *Barbecues,* led by Tommy Darling. In 1968, Underground music started becoming popular and one of the first bands to play this in Ghana was the *Super Eagles* from Gambia. The first Ghanaian band to play the music of Jimi Hendrix and Carlos Santana was the *Aliens,* formed in 1968. Below is a list of favorite bands in Ghana, taken from the magazine *Afro-Rhythms* of August 1968.

1) Akwaboah's guitar band from Kumasi
2) *Armed Forces Band* at Burmah Camp Accra
3) *Avengers Band*
4) *Black Beats* of King Bruce
5) *Black Santiagos,* which played Congo music, under the leadership of Ignace de Souza
6) E.T. Mensah's *Tempos,* by then playing Abela Highlife, Congo music, and Pop
7) *El Pollos*
8) *Heartbeats*
9) Onyina's guitar band from Kumasi
10) *Ramblers,* a dance band led by Jerry Hensen
11) *Shambros,* a dance band at the Lido specializing in Pachangas, with their lead singer Olympia
12) *Uhurus,* a dance band led by Stan Plange
13) *Workers' Brigade Band No. 2,* a sixteen-piece band led by Prince-Boateng.

Pop bands also started appearing in Nigeria in the early sixties, and the earliest ones, as in Ghana, were composed of students and schoolboys: for instance, the *Blue Knights* and the *Cyclops,* based in Lagos. They were given impetus by the visit of Millicent Small (Millie) and Chubby Checker in 1967. By 1968, Soul made an appearance in the country with the first live band being the *Heartbeats.* This led to a number of Nigerian Soul bands being established: for instance, the *Hykkers International,* Tony Benson's (Bobby Benson's son) *Strangers,* which played at the Caban Bamboo, and Segun Bucknor's *Soul Assembly.* Segun had formed a schoolboy Pop band called *The Hot Four* in 1964 and in 1968 formed his *Soul Assembly,* which released on record his Soul compositions "Lord Give Me Soul" and "I'll Love You No Matter How."

The Change

Around 1970 a great change occurred in the popular music of West Africa, both among the student-oriented Pop bands and the Folk guitar bands. Most important is Afro-beat, pioneered by Nigeria's Fela Anikulapo (Ransome) Kuti. He had originally been the leader of the Jazz-Highlife group, *Koola Lobitos;* but in 1970, after a visit to the United States, he changed the band's name to *Africa '70* and brought out his new Afro-beat sound, a fusion of African music, Jazz, and Soul. His first release was the single "Chop and Quench," which was an immediate success. This music has had a tremendous influence in liberating Pop bands from their emphasis on Copyright music, or music imitative of Western Pop records. I should add that Fela's revolutionary approach was anticipated by the famous Ghanaian drummer Guy Warren (Kofi Ghanaba), who as early as the mid-fifties was developing a style of African Jazz. Unfortunately he was too far ahead of his time and, although his "Afro" style became popular with black Americans, it did not catch on in West Africa.

Concurrent with the rise of Afro-beat has been the revival and revitalization of West African guitar-band music. In Nigeria there is the modernized Juju music of Sunny Ade and Sonny Okosun's Rock version of Victor Uwaifo's Benin music; in Sierra Leone there is Milo Jazz, an updated folk version of Meringue music; and in Ghana there is a new surge of interest in the Folk Highlife bands, the most popular being the Ga group *Wulomei.*

But let us turn to Ghana and the emergence of Underground music. The first Ghanaian band to play this music was the *Aliens,* led by Ricky Telfer; later came *Blue Magic* and a new band formed by King Bruce called the *Barristers.* By 1970, with Fela's approach catching on, several Ghanaian bands started experimenting with their own "Afro" styles. The *Aliens,* by then known as the *Psychedelic Aliens,* was the first when it released an L.P. which was a cross between Jimi Hendrix and African music.

In Kumasi there was a band called the *Q-Masters,* which had been formed out of a Sierra Leonese group, the *Echoes,* residing in Ghana since 1967. Then, in 1970, they teamed up with the Sierra Leonese guitarist "Papa" Maurice Williams who had been leader of Sir Albert Margai's *Akpata Jazz* and had then gone to Ghana to play with the *Black Santiagos* until it broke up in 1970. The *Q-Masters* created what they called the "Cross-beat," based on the traditional rhythms of the Poro Secret Society of Sierra Leone, with Latin and Pop influences. In 1971, some members of the *El Pollos*' second band, the *Triffis,* went to Nigeria and returned as the *Big Beats.* They were so impressed by Fela there that they brought out their own Ga Afro-beat records. Their most successful effort was their single "Kyenkyenma" ("Decrepit"), which became a catchword in Ghana for anything that is antiquated or not up to date. Another band formed in 1971 was *Sawaaba Soundz,* which specialized in Afro-beat numbers and released several singles.

Besides the influence of Fela, another factor which characterized Ghanaian Pop music was the Soul to Soul concert of March 1971. Tens of thousands of Ghanaians flocked to Black Star Square in Accra to hear Roberta Flack, Eddie Harris and Les McCann, Wilson Pickett, the *Staple Singers,* Ike and Tina Turner, *Santana,* and the voices of East Harlem. Also featured were two Ghanaian bands, the *Psychedelic Aliens* and Kwaa Mensah's folk music ensemble. The *Aliens* opened up the twelve-hour show with their Afro-Underground music and were followed by a very exciting fusion of the modern Jazz of Harris and McCann and the Fra-Fra calabash of Amoa Azangeo from the Arts Council of Ghana. However, the biggest impact was made by *Santana,* whose fusion of Rock and Latin music became a source of inspiration for young Ghanaian musicians. Indeed, "Santana Man" became a current phrase in the country, synonymous with the terms "Afro" and "Psychedelic." King Bruce consequently formed yet another band, the *Barons,* specializing in this style.

A third influence on the Ghanaian Pop scene was *Osibisa,* the name being derived from the old Fanti name of Highlife, "Osibisaba." This London-based Afro-rock band, founded by three Ghanaian musicians who had originally been Highlife musicians (Teddy Osei, Mac Tontoh, and Sol Amarfio), made a tour of Ghana in 1972. That same year saw the formation of two more groups who were moving away from "Copyright" toward their own style. One was *Cosmic Boom* or *Boombaya,* formed by the Bannerman brothers, and now residing in London; the other was *Zonglo Biiz,* which included the drummer Smart Pozo from the old *Aliens,* and the bass player George McBruce, who later went on to join Fela in Lagos. Since 1973 this Africanization of Pop bands has continued with more and more original material being included in their repertoires. In addition, many of the groups have changed their names to more African-sounding ones.

Below is a list of some of the recent Ghanaian Pop groups, excluding the concert guitar bands and the large Dance bands. All these Pop bands play a wide range of music which includes Highlife, Kara-Kara (Congo music), Soul, Reggae, Underground music, "Smoochie-time" ballads and Afro-beats.

1) The *Apagya Show Band,* originally called the *Steneboofs.* Their Afro-rock number "Simigwado" was considered so indecent that it was banned from the radio.

2) *Wantu Wazuri* (Swahili for "Beautiful People"), led by Tommy Darling.

3) *Jewels,* resident band of the Tip-Toe night-club.

4) *Uppers International,* based in Bolgatanga and led by Chester Adams, and featuring the singer Prince Ali.

5) *Blemabii,* a Pop band that turned folk, led by the headmaster Mr. Addy.

6) *Asase-asi* (underground), formerly called the *Los Cubanos*

7) *The Sweet Talks,* managed by Raymond Azziz.

8) *Gee Dees* (formerly the *Q-Masters*).

9) *Sawaaba Soundz* (now called *B Soyaaya*).

10) King Bruce's bands: the *Black Beats, Barbecues, Barristers, Barons, Bonafides, B Soyaaya* and *Boulders.*

11) The three bands of "F" Promotions: *Hedzolleh, Basa-Basa* and *Bunzu.*

12) *Adam's Apple.*

13) *Black Berets,* an army band based at Burma Camp, Accra.

14) *Fourth Dimension,* another army Pop band.

15) *Sweet Beans* led by Pat Thomas and run by the Cocoa Marketing Board.

16) *Ogyataana* ("Flame").

17) *Kukurudu* ("Earthquake").

18) *Alpha-Omega.*
19) *Ionic Revolt.*
20) *Bisa Goma.*
21) *Pagadeja* (from the break-up of *El Pollos*). This band has since left for England where it became known as *Bukutu,* based at Harry Appiah's club in Liverpool.
22) *Boombaya,* residing in London.

The most important music promotions are those of King Bruce, Faisal Helwani and Raymond Azziz. Faisal Helwani's pioneering role in African music I will deal with in Chapter Seventeen. King Bruce is an old-time musician who formed the *Black Beats* in 1952 and now has about seven bands playing mostly "Copyright" music. "Ray Publicity" is a progressive music business owned by Raymond Azziz. From 1967 he managed the *Black Santiagos* and organized a series of Pop chains called "Soul Brother Competitions." He has also promoted bands from other West African countries, namely the *Heartbeats* of Sierra Leone, Fela's *Africa '70,* and Segun Bucknor's *Soul Assembly* from Nigeria. At present he is the manager of a top quality band called the *Sweet Talks* which recently toured with the Ghanaian singer Joe Mensah.

Before closing this section on the recent changes in Ghana's popular music I should add that there is now a definite convergence between two creative movements, the rise of Afro-beat and the revitalization of the less-westernized Folk music. *Hedzolleh* started in the Pop milieu playing Afro-beats, but ended up playing folk songs, like the Liberian song "Rekpete." *Blemabii* started as a group playing *Osibisa*-type Rock and underground music; then, encouraged by *Wulomei*'s success, ended up playing their own local Ga music. On the other hand, musicians like Ampadu of *African Brothers* are absorbing new ideas from Pop and Afro-beat.

The most important factor that has emerged on the Nigerian popular music scene in the seventies is Fela Anikulapo Kuti's Afrobeat and the multitude of bands influenced by him. The only real contenders would be Juju music and the guitar band music of musicians such as Victor Uwaifo and Stephen Osadabe.

Fela's influence has been profound. A good example is Sonny Okosun, a musician who was with Victor Uwaifo in 1969 and 1970,

only to split away to form his own group which plays "Jungle-Rock"—
a combination of Uwaifo-type rhythms, Afro-beat, and *Santana*-style
guitar. The name *Ozzidi* comes from an Ijaw god who was the best
dancer and singer among the gods. Another musician influenced by
Fela was Segun Bucknor whose *Soul Assembly* has already been
mentioned. From Soul music he has moved to more political songs:
for instance, his records "Poor Man Get No Brother" and "Nigeria
One and Forever." From the north of the country, from Kaduna, has
come the *Northern Pyramids,* which plays a Hausa form of Afro-beat.

Since the emergence of Afro-beat, a large number of young bands
have come into existence, each trying to create their own sounds. Typical are the Afro-rock of Berkeley Jones' *BLO* and Johnny Haastrup's
Mono-Mono, which went to America for a time. Another band that
left the country is *Ofo and the Black Company,* formed in 1972 and
playing what is called "Afrodelic Funk." It became the resident band
for a time at Ginger Johnson's Iroku Club in London. Yet another
experimental group that is out of the country is *Twin Seven Seven
and the Black Ghosts.* However, this is not a new group, as it has
been based in America for many years, where its fusion of Ijala
drumming from Oyo and Afro-American music has made a mark.
There are plenty of bands remaining in Nigeria, however, playing
"Afro" music: for instance, the *Shango Babies, Eassy Kabaka,* the
Gondoliers, and *Cicada.* A band based at the Can-Can in Lagos is
Baranta, led by Francis Foster of the *Heartbeats.* A band at the
Granada Hotel called the *Granadians* has developed an Afro-beat
based on the Makossa Highlife music of the Cameroons, since some
of its members were from a band in that country called *Voory's
Power.* I shall deal with Fela himself in a separate chapter.

The situation today with Afro-beat is thus very different from the
days when Highlife was evolving. Then there was a colonial situation
with urban African musicians copying western music (albeit mostly
black American dance music). Today West Africa is independent,
traditional "cultural" music is being given its rightful place, and the
western music that is being assimilated is Black American music
looking towards Africa for inspiration. This has had a liberating effect
on the "colonial mentality" still prevalent with many African Pop
musicians; for, ironically, to copy Western Pop today (i.e. Black
American music) is to turn towards the African roots of this music.

Fela Anikulapo-Kuti at the Africa Shrine in 1974, a few days after a brush with the police

Sixteen

Fela—The "Chief Priest of Afro-Beat"

Fela Ransome-Kuti was born in Abeokuta, Nigeria, in 1938. His father was a Reverend Minister and his mother, Funlilayo Ransome-Kuti, a powerful political lady who came to prominence as one of the leaders of the mass demonstrations by women against the British during the colonial period.

One of Fela's first band stints was with Victor Olaiya in Lagos in which he was the vocalist. In the early sixties he went to London to study music at Trinity College, and formed the *Highlife Rakers* there. He was then playing trumpet and, when he returned to Nigeria in 1967, formed the *Koola Lobitos*—a band that fused Highlife and modern Jazz, and was particularly popular in Ghana, which he visited often. Two of his most successful recordings during this period were the Highlife "Yeshe Yeshe," released in 1967, and "Mr. Who Are You?," released the same year. However, after a ten-month trip to the States in 1969, he changed musical direction, formed his band *Africa '70,* and started developing his Afro-beat, a music that has swept West Africa in the last few years. His first Afro-beat release was the single "Chop and Quench," and since then he has brought out a large number of L.P.s. Below is a list of them.

"London Scene"
"Nai Poi"
"Open and Close"
"He Miss Road"
"Shakara"
"Alagbon Close"
"Gentleman"
"Roforofo Fight" (double L.P.)

113

"Confusion"
"Expensive Shit"
"Kalakuta Republic"
"Everything Scatter"
"Yellow Fever"
"Zombie"

The themes of the lyrics of these records (sung in Yoruba or Pidgin English) concern the problems of modern urban Africa. For instance, in "Gentleman" (EMI 0009), Fela states that he would rather be a natural or "original" African man than be dressed up in a European suit affecting refined manners. "Shakara" (EMI 008N) is concerned with the way modern Nigerians "bluff themselves" in the towns:

"Shakara"

I want to tell you about lady-o,
She go say she equal to man,
She go say she got power like man,
She go say anything man do,
She self fit (can) do . . .
(But) African women go dance, she go dance the fire dance,
She know man na (is) master,
She go cook for am
She go do anything he say,
But lady no be so,
Lady na master . . .

Another song that criticizes westernized Nigerian women is "Yellow Fever," which condemns those who ruin their faces with bleaching soaps. "Confusion" (EMI 004) is literally about the confusion of modern Lagos:

"Confusion"

Them be three men wey (who) sell for road-side-o,
Them three speak different languages-o,
Them three speak Lagos, Accra and Conakry,
One man come pay them money-o,
He pay them for pound, dollars and French money-o,
He remain for them to share-o,

Me, I say no confusion be that-o,
(i.e. it will take them hours to work out the change.)

"Expensive Shit" (SWS 1001) is about a brush Fela had with the police in 1975 during which he was suspected of possessing Indian hemp. The police did not find any on him, so took a specimen from him. The front cover of the L.P. states: "The men in uniform alleged I swallowed a quantity of Indian hemp. My shit was sent for lab test. Result negative which brings us to Expensive Shit." In a later L.P., "Everything Scatter," he praises Kwame Nkrumah, Sekou Touré, and General Amin. One of his most political songs is "No Bread":

"No Bread"

For Africa here, him to be home,
Land boku from North to South,
Food boku from top to down,
Gold de underground like water,
Diamond de underground like sand sand,
Oil de flow underground like river,
Everything for overseas,
Na from here him de come,
Na for here man still de carry faeces for head.

I first saw Fela performing in 1971 when he came to Ghana, and at that time he was playing electric piano and was accompanied on stage by his "Afro-sexy" dancers. The second time was in November of 1974 at his club, the Africa Shrine, at which I was staying with members of *Basa-Basa* and *Bunzu,* two Afro-beat bands from the Napoleon Club in Accra. We were there to record at the EMI studio in Lagos, and Fela was going to help our manager, Faisal Helwani, with the mixing. Unfortunately, the very first morning we were there, Fela's place, which is opposite the Shrine, was attacked by about sixty riot police with tear-gas. They were looking for a girl they claimed had been abducted. (Being so near, we too were gassed.) We didn't see him for about three days, but when he did return, it was in style; for not only had he recovered from the wounds the police had given him, but he also won an Indian hemp case in court. (Fela referred to Indian hemp as NNG, or Nigerian Natural Grass.) He was accompanied by about ten thousand people from the court in Lagos to the Shrine, played there that very night, and helped us with our recordings the next day.

His Shrine is situated in the open court-yard of the Empire Hotel in Mushin, the same hotel that boasted the *Empire Dance Band* in the fifties and sixties (playing Highlife and Ballroom music). Fela's club gets its name from the "Shrine" he has built in the court-yard, dedicated to Kwame Nkrumah. Often Fela, the chief priest, will pour a libation at this shrine before playing.

The following is a typical picture of the Shrine as I saw it in 1974. The stage is "T"-shaped, with Fela out front with his electric piano, and flanked by two musicians playing maraccas and clips. The rest of the band is stretched out behind him. It is a large band, consisting of two trumpeters, tenor and baritone sax players, three guitarists, a trap drummer, and two seated musicians playing hand drums. In front of them but behind Fela are six beautiful girls who provide the chorus. Fela speaks in a mixture of broken English and Yoruba, continuously joking with the audience in between numbers, and they joke back. As soon as Fela is ready he nods to a young man waiting at the wing of the stage who gracefully leaps up to clip the sax on him (this is Fela's latest instrument). Fela waits patiently, not moving a muscle until the microphone is adjusted and everything is set for him; then one, two, three, they are off. He is strict with his musicians, and if any of them makes a mistake or does not concentrate he may fine him on the spot; consequently they have their eyes fixed on him all the time. As they are playing, four "sexy" dancers perform on shrouded raised platforms or podiums. One is at each corner of the dance floor and the girls are silhouetted onto the lace material by colored lights. Fela is in complete control as he uses four foot-pedals to signal any one of the dancers to stop if she tires; then another clambers up to begin.

Fela's home, the Kalakuta Republic, is opposite the Shrine, and his popularity is so great that it needs a tight security system of barbed wire fences, aggressive gate men, and a rather fierce-looking but docile Alsatian to keep out unwanted visitors. Inside Fela rules his kingdom—which includes his musicians, dancers, and a pet donkey and baboon—with a fist of iron. He is so famous in Lagos that whenever he goes out and about people stop what they are doing and shout his name. I saw an example of this at the Surulere football stadium in 1974, during the Jimmy Cliff show. Towards the end of the performance Fela appeared and was spotted by the audience who carried him down the field, where the massive stage was surrounded by a crowd. When they realized who had come they left Jimmy Cliff en masse and charged around the field with Fela on their shoulders. After that the show ended.

Below is an interview I had with Fela at his home, the Kalakuta Republic, on the 22nd of December 1975.

Collins   What first brought you to music?

Fela   It was in the family; my mother, father, and also my grandfather were musicians. My grandfather was playing traditional music on the piano in the 1920s and 1930s, and he did some records for EMI in England. It was religious music and he used African folk songs, and united them to Christian songs to spread Christianity in the Yoruba area of West Africa. He was a preacher and was responsible for making Christianity in the Yoruba country here—which I think is very bad so I have to undo what he has done.

Collins   You mean that is what is motivating you?

Fela   I wouldn't say that I am purposely antagonizing my grandfather but I would say his mistakes are colonial and we are trying to get the colonial thing out.

Collins   Kofi Ghanaba (Guy Warren) said a very similar thing to me once. He said that his father was doing the colonial thing so he had to undo it.

Fela   (Laughter)

Collins   What were the other early musical influences on you?

Fela   At the very early stage I was influenced by Victor Olaiya. I used to sing for him before I went to England. But these types of bands were all colonial, and they had the influence of hymns somewhere or another in their music. It is the Christian influence which cannot really work in African music.

Collins   Yes, I remember last year at the Napoleon Club you told me that Highlife was black Victorian music. But you did play Highlife in the *Koola Lobitos,* though influenced by Jazz.

Fela   Yes, I was influenced by Miles Davis, Coltrane, Thad Jones; I was very much into modern Jazz at that time.

Collins   I also remember at the Napoleon you said you went to America in 1969, and it was there you found your mistakes.

Fela   I wouldn't say mistakes but shortcomings.

Collins   You mean in terms of direction?

Fela   I mean in terms of direction and music both. Africans are confused people you know, because of colonialism, so it's difficult for an African man to really find himself. You see probably half his life he has thought like an Englishman or like a Russian; it depends on where he has had his education. We are all fucked up so we have to get this influence out of our system. It is this influence I call a shortcoming. Because you cannot as an African be influenced by English culture and play African music; it can't work.

Collins   Are you saying it destroys authentic creativity?

Fela   It destroys authentic creativity.

Collins   So in the *Koola Lobitos* you were trying to bring Highlife towards black American Jazz.

Fela   You see, at the beginning my musical appreciation was very limited, but later I opened up to many black artists and I saw that in Africa we are not open, we are not exposed to music. At that time they only let us hear what they wanted us to hear. When you played the radio it was controlled by the government, and the white man played us what he wanted; so we didn't know anything about black music. In England I was exposed to all these things, but in Africa they cut us off. It was after I was exposed that I started using Jazz as a stepping stone to African music. Later, when I got to America, I was exposed to African history, which I was not even exposed to here. It was then that I really began to see that I had not played African music. I had been using Jazz to play African music, when really I should be using African music to play Jazz. So it was America that brought me back to myself.

Collins   Where did you get your rhythms for Afro-beat from?

Fela   I always tell my friends that if we say Africa is the home of rhythm and music, which will have to be accepted sooner or later, it is because Africans have been playing music for millions of years. If Africa is the home of music then anything that comes from the head of an African artist must depict Africa; that's the true African artist. Now if I had been an Asian or Chinese artist then I would have to think and write if I wanted to play African music. But as an African artist it comes to me naturally, spontaneously; and that is the essence of finding oneself.

Collins   But you are more than an African artist; you are a political African artist.

Fela   Oh yes, yes, the political part of it is a necessity! I don't see how African music today can be about what doesn't affect our lives now. Our music should not be about love, it should be about reality and what we are up to now.

You see, if you want love in Africa we have so many women, you don't need it (i.e., romantic songs). Even our music before was for purposes like religion, work, and politics, and so Afro-beat is an occasion for politics because that is the occasion we are in now—people suffering.

Collins   You call your house the Kalakuta Republic. Could you tell me where you got this name?

Fela   It was when I was in a police cell at the C.I.D. headquarters in Lagos (Alagbon Close); the name of the cell I was in was named "The Kalakuta Republic" by the prisoners. I found out when I went to East Africa that Kalakuta is a Swahili word that means "rascal." So, if rascality is going to get us what we want, we will use it; because we are dealing with corrupt people, we have to be "rascally" with them.

Collins   Could you tell me your plans for the future?

Fela   I want to have a press. My main plan is to extend my communication system so I can reach as many people as I can—across Africa at first, as I'm not interested in Europe right now.

Collins   Will you be involved in the Black Arts Festival?

Fela   Oh yes, I'm very cool with this government. We feel that we are going to progress now because this government sees the sense of having a change. So we are with them and we will support the Festival.

Since the time of this interview Fela has abandoned his middle name, Ransome, which he considers colonial, and has replaced it with the Yoruba name "Anikulapo"—"a man who has captured death in his pocket." His latest project is the production of a full length feature film called "The Black President," scripted by Alex Oduro. It is the story of Fela's life, shot in Nigeria and Ghana, and financed by himself, Faisal Helwani, and Decca. The film starts with his schoolboy days in Abeokuta and ends up with him being led off to prison on an Indian Hemp charge (it is only since the coup of 1975 that the heavy sentences imposed in Nigeria on people possessing Indian hemp have been reduced to moderate fines).

In February 1977, just after the end of FESTAC (the African Arts Festival), Fela's Kalakuta was burned to the ground by members of the Nigerian army, in retaliation for attacks on them by some of Fela's entourage.

Faisal Helwani (left) and Alex Oduro, producers of Fela Anikulapo-Kuti's film "The Black President"

Seventeen

"F" Promotions

Faisal Helwani was born in Sekondi on the coast of Ghana on March 27th, 1946, and was brought up in Ghana. By the time he was eleven years old he was running an ice-cream factory in Swedru, and by eighteen he was in the music promoting field. The following is a brief description of the first shows he promoted.

"I got a dance at the Lido night-club in 1964 with five bands—the *Shambros, Black Santiagos, Ramblers, African Rhythmaires,* and *Ghana Armed Forces Band*—all professional. Until then, every night there were the same monotonous dances with one band playing for six hours from nine to three in the morning. I wanted to introduce show business where there would be competition. Like, at the second Lido show, I made Rim Obeng from the *Armed Forced Band* sit on one side of his drum and Mac Hammad sit on the other, and each would take a solo in turn. Also I used to put up beauty contests and fashion shows. A lot of my activities then were covered by television."

By 1966 Faisal was organizing student "Pop chains" and promoting school-boy bands like the *Thunderbirds*. In 1968 he promoted his own group called the *El Sombraros* under the leadership of Johnny Acheampong and Alfred Bannerman. He first met Fela Anikulapo-Kuti in 1967, and below explains how it happened.

"I then had an electrical hardware shop and, as I had started promoting, I went down to Nigeria to look for some good bands to bring to Ghana. My first time in Lagos was with Chris

123

Ukoli of the West African magazine called *New Breed*. He came to Ghana and watched one of my shows and invited me to his show in Lagos, and there I went out visiting clubs. Then Fela was at a place called the Kakadu playing Afro-jazz songs like 'Yeshe Yeshe,' with Yoruba words but a jazzy beat. So I was introduced to Fela by Chris, and I talked to Fela about coming to Ghana. The next day I went to his house where his mother-in-law and wife were staying (now the Kalakuta Republic) and he agreed to come for £150 a week, and I paid for all accommodations. He didn't have any amplification so when he came I also hired the equipment for him. I took him all over Ghana: Koforidua, Cape Coast, Swedru, Takoradi, Kumasi, Akim Oda, everywhere. Nobody knew him at that time. He was then playing trumpet and his band was called the *Koola Lobitos*. I promoted the record 'Yeshe Yeshe' and went into business with Fela. With Fela I never made any money, but Fela liked Ghana and kept coming."

Fela came again in 1968 for another tour organized by "F" Promotions and, according to Johnny Acheampong, whose *El Sombraros* toured with Fela on that trip, Fela had already started experimenting with a new sound he called Afro-soul and Afro-beat. It is interesting to note that this music became popular in Ghana before it caught on in Nigeria.

In 1968 Faisal organized his most ambitious tour which was a one-and-a-half month tour of East Africa by the *Uhurus* dance band (led by Stan Plange), the *Rolling Beats* dance troupe, and the ace drummer Kofi Ghanaba. After this he opened a night-club which he called the Pagoda (renamed the Napoleon in 1973). Instead of simply turning it into a discotheque, as so many other night-club owners were doing, he took the imaginative step of setting up a resident band there which would specialize in a combination of African music and Pop. It would be a stage more African than *Osibisa*. Thus in October 1973 he formed *Hedzolleh*, which means "peace" or "freedom" in Ga. The composition of the band is as follows:

1) The leader of the band, who plays bass guitar and African xylophone, was Stanley Todd (a Ewe) from the *El Pollos* Pop

group. He replaced Lash Laryea from the *Aliens,* who was the original bassist but had gone to England.

2) Talking drums played by Okyeremah Asante (an Akan).

3) Cow bells and calabash played by Acheampong (an Akan), who came from the *Ananse Kromian Sounds,* the excellent cultural group from the Arts Council of Ghana.

4) Bass Congas played by Morton (a Ga), from the Arts Council.

5) Calabash and drums played by Nortey (a Ga).

6) Lead guitar played by Jagger (a Ga) from the *Aliens.*

7) Bamboo flute played by Nii Lee Ampoumah (a Ga), also from the Arts Council.

This band was out-doored at the Orion cinema in November 1973, played for the Asantehene in December, won the small dance-band competition organized by the Arts Council the same month, and played for the Ga Mantse (Chief) at his palace in January 1974. They also supplied 70% of the soundtrack for the film "Contact," a joint product of the Ghana Film Corporation and the Ital-Victoria company of Italy. About this time the South African trumpeter Hugh Masekela joined the band, and in December 1973 it went to the E.M.I. studios in Lagos to record the L.P. "Introducing *Hedzolleh.*" One of its most popular numbers was "Rekpete," an old Liberian sea shanty which was released as a single. Early in 1974 the band left with Faisal for the United States, but, as Faisal explains in an interview with the *Ghanaian Mirror* (February 7th, 1975), things did not turn out so well.

"I founded, created, financed, managed, produced, and arranged them for recording. On top I organized the Masekela-*Hedzolleh* tour of the United States. In all, I broke through the universal market with *Hedzolleh* within the short period of one and a half years . . . Hugh Masekela showed up in Accra and was introduced to me by Fela Ransome-Kuti, my friend. At that time *Hedzolleh* was already a champion band of Ghana and they had won a contract for the soundtrack of "Contact." In fact, the group was ready to launch into the world market with or without Masekela. I never dreamed that Hugh

Masekela, with the political awareness from the South African experience, would ever try to do this to his fellow black men. So we decided to go on the United States trip together. The whole outfit was financed by me. This included the booster show we put up for Masekela in Accra . . . After the Ghanaian Ambassador for the United States had given us a reception at the Kennedy Arts Center, the way had been paved for full houses wherever we went. We got to Philadelphia and the poster at the entrance of the club where we were playing read "Hugh Masekela." There was no mention of *Hedzolleh* at all; the American pressmen had been brainwashed to believe that the hit record *Hedzolleh* cut with Masekela was actually recorded in South Africa. It was that bad! . . . I decided to come back."

Just before *Hedzolleh* left, Faisal decided to form another band to play at the Napoleon. This band was *Basa-Basa,* which means "pandemonium" in Ga, and specialized in a combination of Rock and Ewe Agbadza. The membership was as follows:

1) Leader and lead guitarist, Francis Eyeye, or Wallace (a Ewe).

2) Cowbells and congas, the Ewe identical twins Joseph (Ringo) and Charles Nyarko.

3) Bass player Nii Ayitey II (a Ga), who had been with *Kukurudu* and *Adam's Apple.*

4) Bass conga Jerry James Lartey (a Ga), who had been leader of the *Expensive Diamonds* of the Caprice Hotel and replaced *Basa-Basa*'s original congaist Slim, a merchant seaman.

5) Talking drums: some months after the band was formed, Ballo Apotey Tabahum was brought in from a Ewe village to play the indigenous Agbadja drums.

6) Fra-Fra calabash was played by Amoa Azangeo from near Bolgatanga, who was originally with the Arts Council and played at the Soul to Soul concert with Eddie Harris and Les McCann. The fusion of the Ewe Agbadza beat with the Fra-Fra music was one of the most exciting features of *Basa-Basa.*

In April 1974 Faisal formed yet another band for his club, but, in this case, it concentrated on Highlifes. He called this band the *Bunzus* but, in fact, the bandsmen had been together for some years playing with concert guitar bands from Kumasi, such as Kwakye's *Music Mayors, Happy Brothers,* K. Frempong's *Cubanos Fiesta,* Oko's band, and Mike Ofori's *Dominos.* They made a one-year tour of Ghana, the Ivory Coast and Upper Volta with the *Cubanos Fiesta.* From Kumasi they left for Accra where they were known as *Asase-asi* and then the *Los Cubanos,* finally ending up in the Napoleon. The composition of the band was:

1) Leader and lead guitarist, Cliff Eck from Larteh.
2) Alto congas, Kojo Eck, Cliff's brother.
3) Cowbells, Eddie Agyepong from Koforidua.
4) Bass guitarist, Paul (a Ewe).
5) Flute, calabash and organ, Yram Hussoo, or Spanky (a Ewe).
6) Bass congas, Jerry Ofori from Accra.
7) From June 1974 I joined the band playing harmonica.

During 1974 and 1975 these two bands played almost every night at the Napoleon, with *Bunzu* starting at eleven o'clock and *Basa-Basa* from one in the morning until three; after this the club remained open as a discotheque until the early morning. As can be expected, this club became the focus for night people and musicians from Ghana and abroad.

The bands also played at a number of charity shows: for example, they played at Nsawam prison, Kumasi Central prison, and Ussher Fort in September 1974. To take an example, we played in the 16th-century Ussher Fort to about four hundred male prisoners, all wearing drab white shorts and smocks or blue cloths. At first the audience was rather subdued, for this was the first time a live band had played in a Ghanaian prison, but by the time we had finished they were dancing "Bone to Bone" (man to man) and were roaring with laughter at the Nigerian comedian Ajax Bukana with his top-hat, tails, odd socks, and long pointed shoes. By the time we left, the audience was really happy and two of the prisoners jammed on the drums, and one was so good that Faisal asked him to come to the Napoleon after he got out of prison.

To go from one extreme to the other, in December of the same year we played for the Head of State, Colonel Acheampong, at a Christmas party in the Castle. Although the audience remained more sedate than those at the prison, the music finally got to them when two officers became so excited they started careening around the lawn to the amusement of all. *Basa-Basa* also played at a concert organized by the Black Brothers International in memory of Kwame Nkrumah, to raise money for the African Liberation Fund in September 1974, and at the Featherweight Commonwealth Boxing Championship held in the Accra Sports Stadium in December.

In November 1974, the two bands went to the eight-track E.M.I. studios in Lagos to record L.P.s and the following is an account of the eleven-day trip I wrote after returning.

"After a sixteen-hour journey to Lagos, a session at Victor Olaiya's Papingo night club at the Stadium Hotel, and finally sleep at the Empire Hotel (Africa Shrine) Mushin, we were woken up on our first morning (the 23rd) by the roar of an angry crowd. From our hotel balcony we could see about sixty riot police axing down Fela's front door, just a hundred yards away. Fela's people fought back so then came the tear gas; and we Ghanaian musicians were down-wind!

We discovered later that he had refused to allow the police to make a routine search of his place and consequently received nine stitches in the head for his trouble. According to the *Nigerian Daily Times* of November 27th, the 'Afro-beat King, Fela Ransome-Kuti, stepped into freedom from confinement again yesterday when the police granted him bail following his arrest after last Saturday's police raid on his home.' The very same day he was released he had to appear in court, and the *Times* continued its report: 'Fela was this morning discharged and acquitted by an Apapa Chief Magistrate's Court on a three-count charge of unlawful possession of Indian hemp.' That day we saw a happier demonstration from our balcony than the one on Saturday; for after the court case a huge crowd followed Fela's cavalcade to the Shrine, causing a massive 'go-slow' of traffic. The same night he played alongside *Basa-Basa* and the *Bunzus,* with one arm in a sling and wearing a skull-cap which he humorously called a 'Pope's hat.' For the days Fela had been away his lawyer sang the vocals and subsequently became known as 'Feelings Lawyer,' as he made such a good substitute.

Faisal most certainly did the right thing when he decided to lodge us at the Shrine, the center of the modern West African music scene. There we met Johnny Haastrup of *Mono-Mono*, who told us he was thinking of bringing his band to Ghana for a tour. Berkely Jones of *BLO* was around briefly and mentioned that he had recruited a new bass player. Big Joe Olodele, who used to be with the *Black Santiagos* in Ghana, is now with the *Granadians*—and Albert Jones from the *Heartbeats '72* was down from his base in Kano. And we had live Juju music every night from the Lido night club opposite the hotel.

Our bands went down very well at the Papingo, where we played four nights alongside the resident *All Stars* (ex-*Cool Cats*). We spent two days in the recording studio where Faisal and Fela were co-producing the session, and Faisal jammed on organ for some numbers. On the 30th of November we all departed, including the midget Kojo Tawia who came as our mascot, leaving Fela and Faisal to mix the recordings. We were meant to play at the Cultural Center in Cotonu on our way back home, but we arrived the day the 'People's Revolution' was declared in Dahomey and found Cotonu deserted; everyone had gone to Abome. We did, however, **play the following night at the Centre Communitaire in** Lome.

We all learned a lot from our short stay in Nigeria. Fela is the top musician there, much more popular than foreign artists such as James Brown, or Jimmy Cliff, who was barely able to pull in a crowd of six thousand at the sixty-thousand capacity football stadium at Surulere on the 28th. A lesson for Ghanaian Pop fans, I think!"

The *Basa-Basa* L.P. was released in 1975 on the Makossa label (the *Bunzu* L.P. is to be released by Decca), so Faisal decided to go one better: form another band, return to Lagos, and record all three.

As the *Hedzolleh* boys had dropped the name when they left Faisal and stayed in America, he decided to reform *Hedzolleh*. He called in the young ace guitarist from Akwapim, Joe Miller, as leader, with Ashela and Willie Quist from Accra on bass, maraccas and vocals. They were backed by four Akan musicians: Richard Corffie on cowbells, Nortey on lead congas, Abeku on bass congas, and Johnny Glover on talking drums. In June 1975, the three bands went to the sixteen-track A.R.C. studio in Lagos (partly owned by Ginger Baker) and recorded more L.P.s with Fela jamming on some of them.

During that year the Napoleon Club itself underwent major renovation and so the club activities had to stop for a time. When it reopened Faisal instituted the successful Monday-night Jazz sessions at which popular musicians like Fela, Victor Uwaifo, Jerry Hansen of the *Ramblers,* Sammy Odoh of the *Black Beats,* Pat Thomas of the *Sweet Beans,* E.T. Mensah, and the Ghanaian blues harmonica player Henry Mills, jammed Jazz numbers, backed by the *Alex Kotey Quintet* from the Ghana Broadcasting Service Orchestra—and *The New Hedzolleh.*

Fela and Faisal have both gone into business with Decca West Africa and as previously mentioned are busily putting together a film of Fela's life called "The Black President," written by the young Ghanaian poet Alex Oduro and co-produced by Fela and Faisal. Decca is supplying the sound equipment and the Ghana Film Corporation is doing the shooting on location in Ghana, Lagos, and Abeokuta. The music from the film will be released by Decca. Faisal has also become the Decca "roving ambassador in Africa" and has already released an L.P. of re-recordings of some of the *Tempos'* most popular hits from the fifties: it is called "E.T. Mensah, the King of Highlife Music." Faisal is now planning to do the same with the Palm-wine guitarist Kwaa Mensah.

In 1977 Faisal started a regular Friday night program on Ghana Broadcasting which he called "Afro-disia Hour." He also started a Wednesday night "Afro-disia night" at the Tip Toe Gardens, at which he featured his three bands, plus groups like the *Uhurus, Abladei Adjo, Bokoor,* and E.T. Mensah. Also that year he took many of these groups, plus Kwaa Mensah and the *Black Angels,* to Lagos to record. Unfortunately a misunderstanding arose between Faisal and Decca and the eleven mastertapes were never released.

Since then Faisal has been an active member of the Musicians' Union of Ghana (M.U.S.I.G.A.), and he was the driving force behind the Great Musicians' March on the seat of government in Accra in 1979.

Basa-Basa, an Afro-beat band from Ghana, at the Napoleon nightclub in Accra

Bunny Mack

Eighteen

Segun Bucknor and Popular Music in Lagos

Segun Bucknor was born in Lagos in 1946 and became interested in music at an early age. At King's College, his secondary school, he was in the school choir, and during his school days he joined and recorded with Roy Chicago's Highlife dance band based in Lagos. In 1964, Segun, Sunni Smart-Cole, and the Nelson Cole-Brothers formed a school Pop band called the *Hot Four*. Then, in 1965, he went to study in the U.S., where he was exposed to Soul music. He returned to Lagos in 1968, by which time the *Heartbeats* and Tony Benson's group were playing Soul. He called his school friends from the *Hot Four* and formed the *Soul Assembly,* which recorded two numbers, "Lord Give Me Soul" and "I'll Love You No Matter How." In 1969 this group was disbanded and then reformed under the name *Segun Bucknor and the Assembly,* which he later changed to *Segun Bucknor and the Revolution.* The *Assembly* (or *Revolution*) did not concentrate exclusively on Soul as did the *Soul Assembly,* and went on to develop their own style of Afro-beat and Afro-soul. Segun shaved all his hair and brought in three girl dancers whom he called the "Sweet Things"; their main venue was the Crystal Gardens. The band recorded many numbers which were influenced by Highlife, Soul, and Jazz. The following numbers are among them: "Poorman Got No Brother," "Abedo," "Sorrow Pass Sorrow," "Son of January 15th" (this was a Soul number and a poetic restatement of post-colonial Nigerian history), "Who Say I Tire" (a satire on Nigerian society), "Love and Affection" (an Afro-rock), and "Pocket Your Bigmanism" (a song against the Nigerian *noveau riche*).

In 1975 Segun disbanded his group and took up journalism. The following is an interview I had with him in his house in Yaba,

133

Lagos, on the 21st of December 1975.

Collins   What first interested you in music?

Bucknor   My family was a family of musicians, as they were church singers or organists. Even right now I have three relatives who are active in music: one is a concert pianist, one is at the Nigerian Broadcasting Company, and one is at Television House. I really started learning music when I was in the second form at school. I must have been nine when I started playing box-guitar and started tinkling around with the piano. Later I was in the school band and choir.

Collins   What sort of music were you playing?

Bucknor   English tunes, classical tunes, and church hymns—and, on our own, we accompanied the current Highlife hits and Pop tunes.

Collins   Which was your first band?

Bucknor   Apart from the school band, I was a solo artist until late 1964 when we formed a band called the *Hot Four*. In 1968, I formed the *Soul Assembly* which even went to Ghana. Then in 1969 I formed *Segun Bucknor and the Assembly.*

Collins   What sort of music influenced you—artists like James Brown?

Bucknor   No, not really. What we did was take all the tunes that were popular at the time, whether they were by black Americans or whatever; but at that time Soul music was the thing. One singer I have always enjoyed was Ray Charles, because I listened to him when I was in the States.

Collins Tell me about the first Pop bands in Lagos.

Bucknor They were school bands, and the first one was the *Blue Knights.* Then the first serious Rock 'n' Roll band we saw was called the *Cyclops;* they were just out of school and formed in 1964. The beginnings of Pop and Rock 'n' Roll were at the United States Information Service (U.S.I.S.), as they had an amplifier and P.A. We used to go there on week-ends but there were no permanent groups, as we would just team up and give ourselves a name. Soul groups like the *Hykkers International* and Tony Benson's *Strangers* came later—around 1968.

Collins What were the main influences on Nigerian Pop music?

Bucknor There were imported Pop magazines like *Mirabelle* and *Fab.* Then we were listening to the records of James Brown, Wilson Pickett, Otis Redding, and Rufus Thomas. Around 1967 Chubby Checker and Millicent Small came, as there was a growing interest in Pop.

Collins Tell me more about the actual Pop bands in Lagos.

Bucknor Around 1964 to 1968 you had people who, even if they were not schooled in music, had the innate talent; they could listen to a record, pick it, play it, and sometimes do it better with their own innovations. The *Hykkers* guitarist was very good, and so was Berkeley of *BLO.* Then around 1970 to 1971 there came an urge, not just to stay and play what you hear on records, but an incentive for compositions. I will say modestly that this trend has been around since 1969 when I started my own band and we were doing our own songs. Then you had band-boys coming up with their own beautiful compositions from *Hykkers, Ofo,* Johnny Haastrup of *Mono-Mono* and Sonny Okosun. Thus, for you to thrive here in Nigeria you have to be very prolific and good at your compositions, even though you have to play a few Pop numbers for the night-club clientele. I've heard it is a bit different in Ghana; there all the night-club audiences want to hear copies of the records they've heard on the radio. However, although there has been a great proliferation of Pop bands, in the last two or three years there has been a decline, and they have faded, due to the steady increase in support for Juju music. I don't think *Wings* and *Hykkers* exist anymore. Johnny Haastrup's group is between life and death, I have stopped active involvement, and *Ofo and the Black Company* are no longer on the scene, as they are overseas. Another thing that created a decline in Pop music has been the rise of the army. Initially they supported groups, as almost every brigade wanted to have a group or band attached to it. They bought instruments and recruited boys; and so they started poaching, which affected the civilian bands.

Collins   You say the main competition with Pop music is from Juju music. Tell me about this music.

Bucknor   It's been going for years and has always been a variant of Highlife, especially the guitar-band type like E.K. Nyame of Ghana. At first Juju music didn't enjoy much popularity because of our rush to look modern. People here were enjoying going to the Highlife bands with all their expensive instruments, so that Juju bands were relegated to the background. In the fifties and sixties, up to 1966-1967, Highlife was the main thing, and most of our Highlife musicians came from the east. But with the war and the crisis most of the easterners went to Biafra and Highlife bands were grounded in Lagos. Some musicians who left were E.K. Arinze, Charles Iwegbue, Zeal Onyia, and Rex Lawson, who was then currently the Highlife superstar. So, there was a dearth of musical entertainers in Lagos, and, since people must have their fun, they turned around to Juju bands. There was a vacuum, since places like the Lido, Empire Hotel, and Kakadu all lost their resident Highlife bands. Only Victor

Olaiya and Roy Chicago stayed, because they were from Western Nigeria. The result is that today ears have been turned to the easy style of Juju, and Highlife is considered to be too rigid and formalized. But, as you know, music can never remain static, and Juju music as it is now has a lot of influences from Pop, Rock, and Afrobeat. For instance, in Obey's last two albums one of his numbers is an old Konkoma number called "Calabar," and another is a Ghanaian Highlife. If someone comes in ten years and looks at Juju music he would probably say it was Pop music, because it's picking up so many of these influences.

Collins   Tell me more about the early music scene in Lagos.

Bucknor   You have to take it on two levels. One was the European influence from the turn of the century with people forming English-style orchestras like the *Lagos City Orchestra;* many of the members today are judges and company directors. Also coming in was the influx of Brazilians and we had a Brazilian Yoruba section of Lagos (like the Gomez family). As a result we had a diffusion of Latin American dance music. On the other hand, by the early thirties you had informal dance-steps like Konkoma. This was not like the dance bands but was what you would now call Highlife, but without the guitar. This dance-step was later called Agidigbo, as it took the name from the Nigerian instrument which is a box with five strings (hand-piano). These groups also used congo-like drums, bongos, and local drums. Later they started adding guitars. This Highlife music was called different names in different parts; in Western State it was called Ashiko and in the Mid-West it was called Konkoma— later it was all called Juju music. So the low-class Konkoma and the E.T. Mensah type of Highlife existed side by side. E.T. Mensah's music was liked by people who took the English way; they were the first middle-class Ghanaians and Nigerians. There was a kind of snobbery in that the man who was in the dance bands felt himself nearer the white man, as he would put on hat, tie, and jacket and would be called to balls and formal occasions. On the other hand, Konkoma Highlife was really informal; during the weekend the laborer or carpenter would form a group and play at naming ceremonies and would start to play for some few drinks, some food and a couple of pounds. While the dance bands tried to be more polished, Konkoma was swinging in its own way and has come out in the world as Juju.

Collins   What are your plans for the future?

Bucknor   After the *Assembly* I changed the name to *Revolution* because I was experimenting with Pop music but using the real basic African beat, the African jungle beat. We sounded like a current group called *Ofege* which uses a similar 6/8 beat called Kon-Kon—the basic West African beat. It's like what *Osibisa* did or what *Santana* did with Latin music and Pop. Before *Santana* there were Latin American groups that were making it, but not that big. But since *Santana* came out with a rock Latin beat, older Latin American musicians are coming up, like Mongo Santamaria, who is a bongo player and is now enjoying some success. You know Latin America's and our music is virtually the same. It's all in 6/8 time but when you play Latin American music you have to double the tempo. However, at the moment I don't operate a band. What is happening now is that I'm not playing publicly, although I am still playing for my own enjoyment. Like you, I write for newspapers and magazines.

Nineteen

Music Unions in West Africa

Before turning to the music unions it is worthwhile to first take a brief look at the position of music in traditional society where it is closely woven into the social structure. Thus, instead of being an isolated event one goes to for recreational purposes as in the West, music in West Africa is an integral part of the social life of the community and is played at nearly all important occasions (both at formal ones like court festivals, kinship ceremonies and rites of passage, and informal ones like story-telling, recreational dances and work-songs).

In addition, the social organization of traditional music is not so specialized as it is in the West. For example, the traditional musician can usually make and repair his instrument, whereas in the West it is virtually impossible to make the instruments without a specialist's knowledge and tools. Again there is less distinction between the audience and the performer than in the West; in fact, the idea of a raised stage physically separating them is an innovation from the West.

Finally, except in the Muslim states, the musician in traditional West Africa is not employed on a full-time basis, since music is simply part of everyone's daily life. The exceptions I mentioned are the professional musicians found in Muslim West Africa, known as Griots. These are groups of musicians, with their wives and children, who do not fit into the local communities, for they wander from place to place hiring themselves out. They are musical specialists and, like other specialist groups such as the blacksmiths, they are of low status and can only marry within their own group.

That they are of low status stands in contrast to the usual position of the musician in traditional Africa, which is an honored one. Thus it seems that when the role of musician is firmly integrated into society the status is high, but when the musician becomes a professional, hiring himself out for money and patronage, his status becomes ambiguous.

A similar situation has occurred with the development of syncretic African music on the coast where dance band and guitar band musicians, working within the money economy, first appeared. Their status is ambiguous, if not positively low, and this is not helped by the guitar being associated with drinking-bars and drunkenness. Although the dance band musician is considered to be a cut above the guitar-bandsman, neither is a profession any parent would encourage a child to enter.

The modern African musician has, therefore, started with three great problems not faced within traditional society. First, his status is low, and, second, he has to obtain expensive musical instruments from abroad—which means that the musician often is not able to own his instruments. This, in turn, has led to the growth of music "middlemen" who buy the instruments and then extract huge profits from the musicians; or they loan money and "bond" them to play during the lucrative cocoa or harvest seasons. Third, when the recording companies first appeared in the thirties and forties, no royalties were paid to the musician for the copyright on his work, but only a cash payment. Thus there eventually developed the need for unions to protect the artists' work.

Ghanaian Unions

In the 1950s an Association of Gold Coast Musicians and, later, a Musician's Union, were formed, but these never got off the ground. Band leaders like E.T. Mensah, Kofi Ghanaba and King Bruce realized their importance, both as to the question of royalties and the organizational needs of the musicians. In this respect these passages from a letter written to the *Daily Graphic* (October 6th, 1958) by E.T. Mensah which he entitled "The Need for a Musician's Union" is of special interest:

A Union of Musicians, of which I am a keen advocate, is

slightly different from a normal trade union. It is a union which comprises both the employer and employee, since both are musicians and look to the union for professional guidance and protection. Its organization is complex because it deals with different grades of musicians. There are professional musicians, that is, people who depend on music for earning their living; and non-professionals. Both have attained different degrees of artistic standards. It will be entirely wrong to consider the professional better than his non-professional colleague . . .

Some of our bandsmen have shown gross irresponsibility both to their leaders and to the bands that have trained them. There have been examples of bandsmen accepting outside contracts with the result that they fail to turn up and play with their own bands. Further, immediately after a new band is formed, or a bandsman has expressed his desire to form one, other bandsmen are attracted, and leave their own bands overnight "for love of money." Such musicians make a mockery of the dance-band business. There is a need to control bandsmen and check such acts; this is one of the reasons why all bandsmen should come together.

By 1961 the climate was right for a new union, for by then the government policy was in favor of seeing all workers unionized. That year a meeting was called at the Accra Community Center to work out the formation of a union. Most of Ghana's notable musicians turned up for this and the proceedings were chaired by two ministers of the Convention Peoples Party (CPP), Techie-Menson and E.K. Dadson. At this meeting a constitution was drafted and a Chairman and National Executive Council elected. The first Chairman was E.T. Mensah and the Executive Council included King Bruce, Saka Acquaye, Kofi Ghanaba, Joe Kelly, Tommy Gripman, and Philip Gbeho (the composer of the National Anthem of Ghana).

The aims of the union were as follows:

1) To ensure the welfare and dignity of musicians and establish codes of conduct.
2) To regulate fees and pay.
3) To control foreign musicians in Ghana.

4) To provide copyrights and royalties. The union would act on behalf of the musicians for negotiation and collection of royalties on all works capable of mechanical and non-mechanical reproduction. The union retained 10% of royalties collected.

5) To promote functions and festivals.

6) To invest resources.

7) To establish music schools.

8) To provide social benefits for musicians.

The union was able to make significant gains. At that time Decca had a recording studio in Accra run by Major Kinder and was paying two pence royalty on each six shilling record; the union was able to double this. Also, foreign performers were taxed; for instance, Louis Armstrong had to pay the union when he made his second trip to Ghana in 1962. At its height the union membership reached about two thousand, had branches all over the country, and was affiliated with the Trade Union Council.

Unfortunately, for several reasons, the union started declining. There was much criticism from the press for forming a union which included both employers (band leaders) and employees (bandsmen). Also, corruption occurred within the organization and money and books disappeared mysteriously. On top of all this, E.T. Mensah, one of the main forces behind the union, went into government service and had to drop into the background. From then on, the Executive Council meetings became less and less frequent, until they ceased altogether.

The concert parties and guitar bands also set up their own union in 1960 when Kobina Segoe, a popular magician, organized the Ghana National Entertainments Association, with twenty-eight groups at the founding meeting in Accra. The meeting elected the following executive members:

Life President: Kobina Segoe (magician and schoolteacher)
Honorary Chairman: E.K. Nyame (*Akan Trio*)
Honorary Vice-Chairman: M.K. Oppon (Kakaiku's band)
Secretary: K.M. Hammond (*Ghana Trio*)
Treasurer: Paa Kwesi (*Golden Stars*)
Financial Secretary: S.K. Ofusu (*Brigade Band*)

Public Relations: Bob Cole (*Ghana Trio*)

Membership was open to all comedians, actors and musicians; below is a synopsis of the main by-laws of the association:

(1) To associate with the purpose of providing a central organization, with intent to promote drama in the country.

(2) To stand as supreme promoter for all concerts in order to eliminate middle-men from this field.

(3) To negotiate with overseas coaches to help improve the standard of the association.

(4) To restrict the entry of foreign or unregistered clubs.

(5) To request that the Ghanaian government introduce the teaching of play-acting in schools and colleges.

(6) To collect royalties from the copyrighted plays with a view toward encouraging the production of films.

(7) To control the management of artists performing on stage, in radio, television, films and gramophone recordings.

(8) To give benevolent and charitable aid: such benefits as interest-free loans for concert equipment, sickness benefits, help with funeral expenses, paid education for members' children, and loans for house-roofing.

(9) To earmark 25% of the net profits for the Ghana Arts Council, the "poverty-stricken association."

The organization used sanctions such as fines, suspension, or expulsion to keep discipline and prevent such crimes as fighting, drunkenness, gambling, divulging the association's secrets, bringing sectarian or political tendencies into the club, and inducing members to leave one concert group for another.

Unfortunately the union started to collapse; for it was unable to break the grip of the middle-men, and the promised government help never came. The final blow came in 1966 when the union was dissolved by the National Liberation Council (N.L.C.), which overthrew President Nkrumah, and the new government put a three-week ban on the movement of all concerts.

During this period and the Busia government (1969-1972) that followed, no attempt was made to reorganize the music unions. Finally, in December 1974, a dance band union was set up and the following is an extract from the *Ghanaian Times* (September 28th) of a press conference held to publicize the inauguration of the union:

> A new musical union is born. It is known as the Music Union
> of Ghana and has Jerry Hansen of the *Ramblers International*
> dance band as its President. Major R.B. Larbi of the Ghana
> Armed Forces is the first Vice-President, with Stan Plange as
> Second Vice-President. The Secretary of the union is Don
> Quarcoe of the *Black Beats* dance band; and Harry Mouzalas,
> a journalist, is second secretary. The union has Mr. J. Allotei
> Cofie as its legal advisor, and the untiring Faisal Helwani,
> managing producer of *Hedzolleh, Basa-Basa,* and *Bunzu,*
> as the founding member.
>
> At a press conference held at the Napoleon nightclub, Jerry
> Hansen outlined the aims and objectives, saying the union
> would cater to the welfare of professional musicians and
> protect their performing rights. This, he explained, would
> bring peace and harmony between nightclub owners and
> recording companies on the one hand, and musicians on the
> other. Jerry Hansen said the union will also help promote
> research into indigenous music in general so as to affiliate
> with recognized international unions. In a bid to encourage
> the development of good musicianship in the country, the
> union will also provide a forum for discussion of problems of
> all musicians and raise funds for the establishment of
> institutions to train young musicians in the country.

Just as the dance bands have recently set up a musicians' union,
so the guitar bands and concert parties have done likewise. The
Ghana Arts Council has formed the Ghana Concert Parties Union
with E.K. Dadson as President and J.A. Arthur as Vice-President.
Then in 1976 plans were made to form the Ghana Co-operative
Indigenous Musicians Society (GHACIMS). An executive council was
formed which included such popular concert personalities as Dr. K.
Gyasi, Kwaa Mensah, E.K. Nyame, Ampadu, Onyina, and Love
Nortey. Marathon shows were held in Kumasi, Accra, and Tema in
April 1976 and February 1977 to finance the union, with over forty
bands participating. In addition to the usual functions of a musicians'
union, they hoped to build their own recording studio, co-operatively
owned by the members, and in this way bypass the middle-men who

have plagued the profession for so long. The Union was officially launched during Easter of 1977 and has gathered very large support.

Nigerian Unions

The Nigerian Union of Musicians (N.U.M.) was formed in 1958 with Bobby Benson as the first President, but by the time the year was out he had left. Stan Plange, a member of the executive council, explains why:

> Some of the members decided that they wanted a full-time secretary and they brought in a trade unionist by the name of Amaefule Ikoro, who was to become later the General Secretary of the Nigerian Trade Union Congress (T.U.C.). Although he wasn't a musician he was with the Union for about three years. In fact, Bobby didn't disagree with the idea of getting a full-time secretary, but didn't want him to be one of the trustees who signs checks on behalf of the union. However, Amaefule insisted that he must be one of the trustees or he couldn't file his report to the T.U.C. (the N.U.M. was affiliated with the Nigerian T.U.C.). Bobby disagreed and said that he was just an employee of the union.

After Bobby left, Chris Ajilo, leader of the *Afro-Cubanos Band*, became the President, with Zeal Onyia as Vice-President, Stan Plange as Treasurer, and Amaefule Ikoro as Executive Secretary. The basic objectives of the N.U.M. were as follows:

> (1) To consolidate the unity and organization of musicians and promote their interests in every conceivable way.
> (2) To establish for members decent contract terms, improved earning-rates and job security.
> (3) To insist that all orchestra leaders only sign contracts approved by the union before permitting the services of registered musicians, on a salary stipulated as N.U.M. minimum (the N.U.M. catered to dance bands only).
> (4) To maintain a closed-shop system, making it unworkable for any musician outside the membership of the union to be hired.
> (5) To ensure that compositions and recordings, including

royalties, are appropriately paid for.

(6) To classify bands and musicians according to artistic capacities and to eliminate imitation of compositions and lowering of musical standards fostered by sheer commercialism and other customary pressures.

(7) To contribute towards originality; to provide and maintain a music-school; and to offer and sponsor music scholarships and promote research possibilities on national music.

(8) To arrange exchanges with foreign bands.

In 1960 a rival union was formed by Bobby Benson and Victor Olaiya. Below Stan Plange explains how it came to be formed:

It was formed around August 1960 when preparations for Nigerian independence were going on. The Nigerian government was intending to invite Edmundo Ros to come down and play at the National Independence dance, as Princess Margaret was coming, and we understood she liked Edmundo Ros. Victor Olaiya's band was to play second band. So the Nigerian musicians' union organized a demonstration to protest against the bringing of a foreign group. About eight or nine hundred of us marched with placards from the Empire Hotel, Idioro, to Government House to petition the Prime Minister Tafawa Balewa. Myself, Zeal, Chris and Amaefule went inside and we told him that the contract should be given to the union which would then form a mass band and select musicians to form a national orchestra for the Independence Dance; he agreed and gave the contract to the union. The other union was formed at this time. In fact, I wouldn't call it a union as such; it was a get-together between Bobby and Victor so that the contract wouldn't be taken away from Victor's band. They were out to create the impression that there was another union. So at the Independence Dance the musicians' union and Victor Olaiya played.

Stan Plange left Nigeria in 1961 and the union was still going strong but, as he explains, by about 1965 the union was dead:

I left in 1961 and the N.U.M. was still going. Then Zeal Onyia left for Germany in 1964. I was in Lagos in 1964 and I met some of the musicans, but I think the union was dying. Then, in the latter part of 1965, I was in Lagos with the *Uhurus* dance band, and I didn't meet the union, although I did meet Bayo Martins, who had just returned from England, and he told me he was forming a Musicians' Foundation. But I didn't realize that it was a union; I thought it was a musicians' club and research thing. Since the time of the N.U.M. and Bobby's faction new unions have sprung up but I don't think they have any connection with the earlier unions. You know, there's always been a split in the Nigerian musicians' union, and I can't remember when there was one united union for as long as six months.

Stan Plange seems to be right about the splits that have plagued the history of music unions in Nigeria, for they were split again later, with Victor Olaiya and I.K. Dairo of the Association of Nigerian Musicians on one side and Bayo Martins, Bobby Benson and Fela Anikulapo-Kuti of the Musicians' Foundation on the other. Below are some edited extracts from the Lagos musical paper *Gong* of November, 1974, which highlights some of the differences between these two unions:

"Musicians at War"

Nigerian musicians are at war with themselves. The two major musicians' bodies are at daggers drawn, each accusing the other of vices ranging from imposition and misrepresentation, to lack of organization and ignorance. In the center of the battle are Mr. Isaac Kehinde Dairo, popular Juju musician and President of the Lagos branch of the Association of Nigerian Musicians, and Mr. Bayo Martins, ace drummer and secretary of the Musicians' Foundation. Mr. Dairo described the Musicians' Foundation as irrelevant. He said that its members and officials are non-practicing musicians and therefore have no right to represent Nigerian musicians. He said they are all businessmen wanting to make quick bread from the sweat of musicians, and ours is the only body that represents the Nigerian musicians. There are about 4,000 members of the Lagos State branch alone. Mr. Martins described the Association as "bogus, unprogressive and not happening." He then threw a barrage of questions. How can an association of a national nature be holding its meetings in Yoruba? How can a union which is supposed to fight people's causes be handled by part-time officials? How can an association which should handle labor relations have the main employees of labor (i.e. music promoters and businessmen) not only as members, but as leading officials? Nigerian musicians should have a dynamic body with a good secretariat and a trade unionist as full-time secretary. He said the incessant attacks on his Foundation stem from ignorance of the so-called officials of the Association. He said he recognized their union, as it was one which played a distinct role from that of the Foundation. "All over the world," he said, "musicians' unions exist as trade unions. They handle labor relations, and they are not substitutes or rivals to foundations, which exist as lobby groups to fight the cause of musicians at a governmental level." Mr. Martins explained that his Foundation doesn't seek to represent musicians as a body. "Our relationship with musicians is on a clientele basis, not on a membership basis. We are a business enterprise of a kind."

In 1981 this schism was bypassed by the formation of the Performing Artists Association of Nigeria, by the country's top artists from all fields of music: Sunny Ade, Ebeneezer Obey, Sonny Okosun, Christie Essien, Niko Mbarga, Victor Uwaifo, Bobby Benson and Laolu Akins. The principle aim is to stop pirating, which controls 60% of the Nigerian music market.

In Ghana there has been no need for a new organization as MUSIGA has gone from strength to strength in the last few years (its membership is now over five thousand). The union has helped organize trips to Ghana by international stars such as Mick Fleetwood and Brian Eno, and is currently involved with the government's "Cultural Revolution."

Twenty

The West African Recording Business

The African record industry began in South Africa at the beginning of the century, expanding into West Africa in the late twenties. During this time the major recording companies were Pathe, Zonophone, His Master's Voice (H.M.V.), Columbia, Decca, Brunswick, Edisom Disc, and Polydor. Below is a table of Zonophone and H.M.V. sales in the whole of Africa from 1927 to 1929:

Sales of H.M.V. and Zonophone Records

Year	Whole of Africa	South Africa	East and West Africa
1927-28	1,202,697	1,020,605	182,092
1928-29	1,380,614	1,119,764	260,850
1929-30	1,260,260	876,276	383,984

The figure in the last column for the year 1927-28 represents records sold mainly in East Africa, as very few West African records were pressed by the two companies concerned before 1929. After 1928 they experienced a major improvement when the United Africa Company (U.A.C.) became their distributor and greatly expanded their sales in the West African market. The breakdown for record sales and values in East and West Africa in 1930 are: East Africa, 202,500 (£17,800); and West Africa, 181,484 (£16,000).

By 1930 the West African record trade was so important to Zonophone that it brought out a 35-page record catalogue for that market. Included were the early "3000" series of Yoruba and Ewe hymns and Ewe traditional music, and the later EZ series which included songs in eighteen West African languages. Incidentally, the first in the EZ series was a Dagomba Highlife recorded by a Fanti band in 1925. EZ 1 is therefore probably the first Highlife ever recorded.

After 1930 the record industry kept expanding in West Africa, and between 1930 and 1933 close to 800,000 records were sold by all the companies for a total sales value of £70,000. In 1931, Zonophone, H.M.V., Parlophone, Columbia and Regal combined to form Electrical and Music Industries (E.M.I.) which became the largest recording company on the continent. Its nearest rival in the thirties was the American-based R.C.A., which bought out the Victor label in 1929.

Then in 1939 came the Second World War, and the number of African records being pressed was drastically reduced, as vinyl was needed for the war effort. (During the war, world-wide record production remained low and E.M.I., for instance, which had been producing a fifth of the world's records, had to convert its main factory outside of London to munitions production.) After the war, of course, record production started up again, so that by the 1950s, 78-rpm records of European and African music were pouring into Africa from abroad.

E.M.I. had developed several special labels in Africa: the H.M.V. Yellow label JZ series for the West African market (songs in Twi, Hausa, Yoruba, and Ga). In Ghana, the H.M.V. Taymani Special, a label run by a Lebanese businessman who was also E.K. Nyame's manager, was important. In both the Ghanaian and Nigerian markets there was H.M.V.'s JL and JLK series which recorded Ghanaian groups such as Kwaa Mensah, E.K. Nyame, the *Gold Coast Police Band,* Yebuah, *Mireku,* and Kakaiku, in addition to Nigerians such as E.C. Arinze. A subsidiary of E.M.I., distributed by the Swiss African Trading Company (Parlophone Odeon), released Nigerian artists on their Primrose label PO 5000 series.

Decca, a British company, was also active in Africa after the war, and its distributors in West Africa were the Sociètè Commerciale de l'Ouest Afrique and the Africa Picture Company. In 1947 the Decca West Africa series started up in Ghana, that year seeing production of 46,000 copies of 23 records sung in vernacular languages. By 1952 the Decca label (through its WA, GWA, and NGA series) had produced almost 100 78-rpm recordings of Ghanaian artists, including E.T. Mensah, the *Black Beats,* Onyina, the *Builders*

Brigade, Broadway, the *Red Spots,* Gyasi's guitar band; and also such Nigerian artists and groups as E.C. Arinze, Haruna Ishola, the *Rio Lindo Orchestra,* the *Archibogs,* the *Empire Rhythm Orchestra,* and I.K. Dairo were given recordings, as were musicians from Sierra Leone like Calender and his Maringa group.

During the 1960s the ten-inch 78s began to disappear, to be replaced by the stronger and more economical seven-inch 45-rpm discs, but for a period the record companies were producing both together. For instance, E.M.I. Nigeria's H.M.V. NH and LON series were produced in both formats. Decca also started changing over to 45-rpm production in the 1960s when the 45WA, 45GWA, and 45NWA series replaced the 78-rpm series. In fact, by the late 1950s the West African trade had become so successful that Decca built a recording studio at Winneba, near Accra. In Nigeria, Decca was sending two recording engineers to Yaba in Lagos twice a year to record on a portable machine. During the 1960s Decca West Africa was producing one quarter of a million records a year, mostly singles.

The first pressing plant in Africa was in South Africa, built during the early 20th century. The second was in Nigeria, built by Phonogram in Lagos in the early 1960s. Later Phonogram built a new studio in Onitsha, which was destroyed during the Nigerian Civil War. E.M.I. built its second African factory in Jos, Nigeria (its first being in South Africa), in 1963.

Today the main record companies catering to the huge local market in Zaire and Francophone West Africa are Decca, Philips-Phonogram, and WEA Fillipachi. Decca has recently brought out an 83 page catalogue of African records and cassettes. WEA has set up an office in the Ivory Coast and has organized a series of 32 African concert tours called "Africa Special." Paris-based companies doing African music are Pathe Marconi, now on the decline, Sono Disc, and Safari Ambiance. A local pressing plant was set up by the Sociètè Ivorienne du Discs in Abidjan.

Generally the record business started later in the French-speaking countries and, except for Zaire, which has several multi-national plants, most of the Francophone West African countries only have small studios and pressing plants for 45-rpm singles. Guinea Bissau has one studio; Senegal is soon to open a multi-track studio and pressing plant; Mali, Niger, and Upper Volta have no facilities at all.

Much of the pressing is still done in France and the record industry in Francophone West Africa is well behind the English-speaking countries like Nigeria which have a longer-established local record market. For example, the 13th International Annual Trade Fair of Record and Musical Productions (MIDEM) held at Cannes in 1979 was attended by only three African producers, coming from Nigeria, South Africa, and Algeria—none from Francophone West Africa.

The main recording companies in the English-speaking countries such as Ghana, Nigeria, and Sierra Leone have been English-based companies like Decca and E.M.I. However, today things have changed and there are now many local companies. In the case of Nigeria, the local factor is dominant with even the foreign multi-nationals like E.M.I., Decca, and Philips, 60% Nigerian-owned.

At the moment there are studios and pressing plants in Liberia, Togo, the Ivory Coast, and Sierra Leone. In Ghana there are three 8-track recording studios: one in Kumasi (Ambassador), and two in Accra (Ghana Films and Studio One). There are also two pressing plants in the country: Ambassador Records, a Ghanaian-owned company, and the Record Manufacturers of Ghana, 50% of which is owned by Polygram. Polygram, incidentally, was created in 1972 by the merger of German Polydor and Dutch Philips-Phonogram, and today employs 12,000 people in 30 countries. Between 1969 and 1977 Polygram did 8.9 million cedis of trade in Ghana, and made a profit after tax of almost one million cedis.

In Nigeria, Polygram, Decca, and E.M.I. have 16-track studios and all plan larger ones. There is a 16-track studio in Lagos that Ginger Baker helped set up; and a 24-track studio was recently opened near Ibadan in 1979 by the Nigerian Apala King Haruna Ishola. There are three major pressing plants in the country: Phonogram (Philips) Nigeria Limited, which is 60% Nigerian-owned; Record Manufacturers of Nigeria, in which Decca and E.M.I. each have 20% shares; and a studio and pressing plant in Ibadan for the local Juju music trade.

In October 1978, Nigeria went one step nearer to complete control of its recording business by banning the import of all records into the country. To supply the huge and booming Nigerian record market (mostly L.P.s) in 1979, 12 million records had to be pressed, of which half were foreign under license and half local Juju, Afro-beat, Highlife, Reggae, and so on. Of these 12 million L.P.s, E.M.I. made about 6 million and Phonogram about 3 million. L.P.s sold at 7 naira, 50 kobo, so the total trade generated was 90,000,000 naira!

The closing of the Nigerian borders to imported records has had several external consequences. One was the closing of the E.M.I. pressing plant in Nairobi in 1978. Some E.M.I. staff were even laid off in Britain. The Decca factory that pressed for Nigeria in Dagenham, U.K., had to close down altogether. One undeserved casualty in all this will be Nigerians and lovers of Nigerian music abroad; they will have to pay more now for Nigerian music.

The problems the Nigerian musicians are facing are enormous. Millions of pirate cassettes are sold in shops and in the streets with their makers' names and addresses openly displayed. Royalties are not really understood and musical compositions are usually sold for lump sums. Copyright has not been enforced and even the Federal Nigerian Broadcasting Company was sporadic in its payment of international performing rights. Its last payment to PRS* was of £10,000 in 1978, before radio and TV became defederalized. Since then nothing has been paid. Without copyright protection at an international standard, Nigerian musicians lose heavily, too, as they have no organization to collect for them for air-play in Nigeria. If their music is internationally recognized and played, international royalties may not be forthcoming.

The record manufacturers are facing a shortage of raw materials, after a boom created by the sudden rise in the international price of oil in the early 1970s. Night pressing (i.e., the illegal use of factories after hours) is another headache for the manufacturers. The multinational companies face an additional problem of paying royalties to its international artists at the standard of 12% of retail price when the Nigerian government has placed a 3% maximum on royalties being paid to foreign artists by Nigeria. So these companies have to make up the 9% themselves.

Facing all those in the Nigerian music business, whether musician, manufacturer, producer, or promoter, is the fact that there has been a shrinkage of the industry due to the slow-down of the oil boom. This

*The Performing Rights Society (PRS) is based in Britain and distributes royalties to musicians for public or recorded performances of their works.

has occurred at exactly the same time the Nigerian record industry has become fully independent. Nigeria now manufactures all records sold in the country, just at a time when there is a shortage of vinyl plastic. In addition, all Nigerian musicians have to record, as well as press, in Nigeria, so lines are forming at the recording studios.

Ghana presents quite a different picture from Nigeria; for whereas in Nigeria there is a contraction in the music business after the boom, in Ghana the boom never came. In the last few years the situation has become critical. For instance, between 1969 and 1975, Record Manufacturers of Ghana Limited was making almost 500,000 singles and 100,000 L.P.s a year with a sales turnover of nearly six million cedis. Since then, with the shortages of raw materials and spare parts, production has been down to quarter capacity.

One serious consequence of this deterioration of the record industry has been that the local music boom of the early 1970s (C.K. Mann, *Wulomei,* Konimo, *Hedzolleh, Big Beats,* etc.) was never properly produced. So, naturally enough, kids in Ghana today have turned to well-produced western Disco music recorded in 24- and even 32-track studios. The Disco craze also kills off live music as well. Music production has become so bad that many Ghanaian musicians have left the country. Those that remain have to face rampant pirating of their records on cassettes, in addition to the fact that Ghanaian radio and TV pay no royalties.

In 1979 things became so critical that the Musician's Union of Ghana, MUSIGA, was forced to hold a vigil and march for recognition. At the evening vigil in March a crowd of 10,000 was present with over 1,000 musicians, a motorcade, three brass bands, and well-wishers. They marched the next day to the seat of government at the Castle where a petition was handed in by Eddie Quansah, Faisal Helwani, Stan Plange, C.K. Mann, Tommy Darling, Sammy Odoh, and Willie Amarfio.

Two weeks after the MUSIGA march the Armed Forces Revolutionary Council staged a coup against the corrupt S.M.C. regime. During the few months of house-cleaning initiated by Flt. Lt. J.J. Rawlings and the young A.F.R.C. members much was done to sort out the record business. The copyright laws were revised and the Prices and Incomes Board (P.I.B.) was revitalized, and large amounts of unpaid taxes and royalties were collected from record manufacturers. The P.I.B. also reduced the retail price of records and cassettes and increased the royalties paid to musicians.

Conclusion

As some of these chapters were written several years ago I would like to conclude by bringing everything up to date.

E.T. Mensah has had a bit of a revival since, in 1977, he released a stereo L.P. of his old favorites called "E.T. Mensah: The King of Highlife." This was recorded in Nigeria and released by Decca West Africa (Afrodisia). Mensah was also active on the Executive Council of the Musicians Union of Ghana but has now transferred his attention to the Greater Accra Musicians Welfare Association, a musicians' self-help organization of which he is the president.

Kwaa Mensah did a one-and-a-half-month tour of the United States in 1975 and is still going strong. He is now an active Inspector of the musicians' union MUSIGA, is empowered to check copyright infringements, and is helping to initiate a series of court cases against record sellers who are pirating songs. He also had a success in 1983 with his song "Kalabule," dedicated to the anti-corruption drive of the government.

E.K. Nyame was the president of the Indigenous Musicians Cooperative (GHACIMS) until his death in 1977. An enormous funeral was held for him at the Community Center in Accra where his body was laid in a golden bed surrounded by guitars. The government donated a large amount of money, dubbing it a State Funeral. Later a wake-keeping was held in the streets of James Town, Accra, where about ten thousand people attended and dozens of guitar bands played. As E.K. Nyame had no wife, one of his concert actors, Kwabena Okine, dressed up as a woman to perform the ceremonial duties of his wife during the wake. (Okine, the falsetto singer in Nyame's band, has recently suffered a severe stroke.)

A very popular guitar band from Sierra Leone is the *Afro-Nationals* which plays a type of music strongly influenced by the Congo music of Zaire, but sung in Mende or Creole. Another sound from Sierra Leone is the "Discolypso" of London-based producer Akie Deen, who has released a string of funky Meringues and Highlifes by Sierra Leonese artists like Bunny Mack and Addy Foster Jones. In 1980 Bunny Mack's "Love You Forever" got into the British charts and became a gold disc in Nigeria.

Two developments have recently occurred in the Juju music scene. First, some Juju artists have gone indigenous, like Ayinde Barrister and Ayinla Kollington, who use no guitars and have created a choral/drum form of Juju called the Fuji System. Second, Juju music has suddenly become popular in the West. Sunny Ade has been signed up by Island records (who managed Bob Marley) and his Afro-beat influenced style was a major success on a tour of Britain and America in 1983. According to Britain's leading Pop magazine, *New Musical Express,* Sunny Ade's show at the London Lyceum in January 1983 was the "most exhilarating yet subtle music heard in London for ages." And for the *Guardian*'s reporter the band's "skills and joyful dedication had the effect of making the panorama of English Rock music look jaded and trite." Even Ebeneezer Obey has moved away from his traditional Juju to a more Pop-influenced style and his records are now being released by a British record company, Virgin Records.

The most important Pop influence on African music over the last few years has been Reggae, and it has had a big effect on some of West Africa's top stars. For instance, Sonny Okosun has been concentrating on Reggae numbers, and released an L.P. called "Fire in Soweto" which topped the charts in Nigeria in 1980. Even bigger from Nigeria is Prince Niko Mbarga's *Rokafil Jazz,* a guitar band from eastern Nigeria whose first album was the West African smash hit "Sweet Mother." This was so popular that it even crossed over to the Caribbean as this song combines Highlife and the double lead guitar of Congo music with a Reggae-type bass line—and with lyrics sung in pidgin English. Even Highlife superstar Sir Victor Uwaifo has begun to experiment with Reggae; namely, on the title track from his L.P. "Five Days a Week Love."

In Ghana the folk revival is still going strong, helped by the fact that the Ghanaian government has launched a cultural revolution and is encouraging the local arts. The *Wulomei*-type of band is still very successful, although some of these Ga cultural groups are now using bass guitar; for instance, *Abladei*. *Wulomei* itself is still producing L.P.s but Naa Ananuwa, the talented lady singer of the group, has split away to form her own group called *Suku Troupe*.

Since my interview with Fela Anikulapo-Kuti at his Kalakuta Republic in Mushin, the building has been burned to the ground. This happened in February 1977, just after FESTAC, the Nigerian black arts festival, had closed. Some of Fela's people had set an army motor-bike on fire and the soldiers from a nearby barracks, already annoyed with Fela because he had just released his "Zombie" album, which poked fun at the army mentality, attacked his home and closed down the Africa Shrine. Unfortunately, the sound track of his just-completed autobiographical film, "The Black President," was in the house at the time and was destroyed. So Fela is now having to re-dub the sound track and has re-opened his Africa Shrine. One of his latest albums, "Coffin for Head of State," is dedicated to his mother who died from injuries sustained during the attack on the old Kalakuta.

In recent years Fela has made a number of successful tours of Europe and had a rapturous reception in France when he played to a packed house of fifteen thousand at the famous Hippodrome in Paris.

In fact, there has been a general interest in African popular music throughout the Western world in the last few years. New Wave musicians were the first to incorporate the sound of Africa with bands such as *The Talking Heads*, the *Piranhas*, *Bow Wow Wow*, and *Adam and the Ants* using African motifs in their music. Composer/producer Brian Eno visited Ghana in 1981 and produced a local band called *Edikanfo* on record. In England, white musicians are joining home-grown guitar bands such as *Orchestra Jazira*, *O.K. Jive*, the *Ivory Coasters*, *Alpha Waves*, and the *Highlife Internationals*.

This interest explains why so many record companies in the West are suddenly releasing African music. Virgin Records, one of Britain's biggest independent labels, has been delving into Congo Jazz and released in 1982-1983 several albums of East African versions of this music. South African music is finding an outlet through London-based companies like Rough Trade and Earthworks. The guitar band music of Sierra Leone is coming out on Akie Deen's Afro-Disco label.

I hope this book has given the reader an introduction to the incredible vitality and diversity in the music of West Africa. For a long time popular local music was frowned on by the older generation. To be a bandsman, especially a guitarist, was considered to be the lowest of the low and not a fit profession for a young man (even less so for a woman). But now there is a feeling of optimism among West African musicians as modern recording studios and manufacturing plants are being opened and music unions are gaining strength—not to mention the new awareness in the West of African music.

This upsurge is reflected in one of the songs of Price Niko Mbarga and his *Rokafil Jazz* called "Music Line." The lyrics begin with a pessimistic father trying to persuade his son to give up the music business, unless he wants to remain poor and single. The song ends with the musician (i.e. Mbarga himself) pointing out that he has made a fortune and gotten himself a wife through his band. The music profession has, in other words, come into its own.

Bibliography

Adedeji, J.A., "Form and Function of Satire in Yoruba Drama," *Odu* (University of Ife Journal of African Studies), 4, 1, 1967.

Bame, K.N., "The Comic Play in Ghana," *African Arts,* 1, 4, 1968.

Beby, Francis, *African Music a People's Art.* Harrap, 1975.

Carrington, J.F., "Tone and Melody in a Congolese Popular Song," *African Music,* 4, 2, 1968.

Charters, Samuel, *The Roots of the Blues.* Quartet Books, 1982.

Chernoff, J.M., *African Rhythms and African Sensibility.* Chicago University Press, 1980.

Collins, E.J., "Comic Opera in Ghana," *African Arts,* January 1976.

_____, "Highlife: A Syncretic Folk Music," *African Arts,* November 1977.

_____, "Post-War Popular Band Music in West Africa," *African Arts,* April 1977.

_____, *E.T. Mensah: The King of Highlife.* Forthcoming from Ghana State Publishing Corporation.

_____, *The Jaguar Jokers: Comic Opera in Ghana.* Forthcoming Ghana State Publishing Corporation.

_____, *Pop Roots: The Inside Rhythms of Africa.* Forthcoming from Foulshams of Yeovil.

Jones, A.M., *Studies in African Music,* Chapter 11. Oxford University Press, 1959.

Lang, I., "Jazz Comes Home to Africa," *West African Review,* IVII, 351, 1956.

Nketia, J.H.K., *Music in Africa.* Gollancz, 1975.

_____, "African Music: An Evaluation of Concepts and Processes," *Music in Ghana,* 2, May 1961.

Mensah, A.A., "The Impact of Western Music on the Musical Traditions of Ghana," *The Composer,* 19, 1966.

Moore, Carlos, *Fela Fela, This Bitch of a Life.* Allison and Busby, 1982.

Oliver, Paul, *The Savannah Syncopators: African Retentions in the Blues.* Studio Vista, 1970.

Smith, E., "Popular Music in West Africa," *African Music,* 3, 1962.

Sprigge, R., "The Ghanaian Highlife: Notation and Sources," *Music in Ghana,* 2, May 1961.

Sutherland, E., *The Story of Bob Johnson.* Anowua Educational Publications, Accra, 1970.

Index

163

About the Author

John Collins studied for his B.A. in sociology and archeology at the University of Ghana between 1969 and 1972. He is also a musician and has played, recorded, and traveled extensively in West Africa with guitar bands, concert groups, and Pop bands. Since obtaining his degree he has been carrying on private research in the history and sociology of contemporary West African folk music and drama. He has written two books: *E.T. Mensah, the King of Highlife,* and *The Jaguar Jokers: Comic Opera in Ghana,* both to be published by the Ghana State Publishing Corporation. He has also published several articles in the American magazine, *African Arts.*

Collins ran his own guitar band, *Bokoor,* for five years, and has now set up Bokoor Recording Studio at Ofankor, near Accra.